W9-ATZ-409

PRAYERS that MOVE MOUNTAINS

JOHN ECKHARDT

CHARISMA
HOUSE

Tyndale House Publishers, Inc., Wheaton, IL 60189. All rights reserved.

Cover design by Bill Johnson

Visit the author's website at www.johneckhardt.global.

Library of Congress Cataloging-in-Publication Data:
Eckhardt, John, 1957-
  Prayers that move mountains / John Eckhardt. -- 1st ed.
      p. cm.
  Includes bibliographical references.
  ISBN 978-1-61638-652-8 (trade paper) -- ISBN 978-1-61638-719-8 (ebook)
  1. Prayer--Christianity. 2. Bible--Prayers. I. Title.
  BV210.3.E28 2012
  242'.8--dc23

2012016547

This publication is translated in Spanish under the title *Oraciones que mueven montañas*, copyright © 2012 by John Eckhardt, published by Casa Creación, a Charisma Media company. All rights reserved.

While the author has made every effort to provide accurate telephone numbers and Internet addresses at the time of publication, neither the publisher nor the author assumes any responsibility for errors or for changes that occur after publication.

19 20 21 22 23 — 10 9 8 7 6
Printed in the United States of America

CONTENTS

Contents

Introduction

BE THOU REMOVED!

> For assuredly, I say to you, whoever says to this mountain, "Be removed and be cast into the sea," and does not doubt in his heart, but believes that those things he says will come to pass, he will have whatever he says. Therefore I say to you, whatever things you ask when you pray, believe that you receive them, and you will have them.
>
> —MARK 11:23–24

WHAT MOUNTAIN ARE you facing in this season of life? Unemployment? Financial problems? Difficult marriage? Illness? Foreclosure? Undefeated sin? Whatever it is, the power lies in you to speak to that mountain and say, "Be thou removed!"

The keys to deliverance, freedom, and the abundant life have been given back to us. Jesus came to return to us our authority in the earth so that we can exercise prayer and faith to bring God's will from the heavenly realm into the earth realm, affecting our lives in the here and now.

The Bible says that you can decree and declare things with your mouth, and they will happen (Rom. 4:17). According to Joshua 1:8, you have the power to make your way prosperous, to mow down the mountains in your way. By meditating and obeying the Word of God, you put yourself in a place of life and blessing. Choice is where your power lies. What you choose to speak and declare needs to coincide with how you live and what you meditate on.

The characteristic of a righteous person is faith in God. You have to know God in order to have faith in Him. The key to moving mountains is really knowing God and dwelling in His presence. The just live by faith in God and do not trust in their own abilities or what someone else can do on their behalf. Jesus said it: "Have faith in God" (Mark 11:22).

Don't lift your problems to such a level that they become your idol. You serve a big God who is faithful to deliver His people out of all their troubles (Ps. 34:17, 19). Walk in faith. Prayer can change things. Worship can change things. Your faith can move mountains. You'll prosper even in bad times. Your prosperity is not dependent on the Dow Jones Industrial Average, NASDAQ, or mortgage rates. Your prosperity is dependent on God. Be a giver. Be a worshiper. Be obedient. Live clean. God will prosper you. God will bless you.

When He put all those plagues on the Egyptians in the land of Goshen, nothing fell on the Jews. They were protected from all the locusts, plagues, and judgment. Ask God to put a Goshen anointing on you. It may be falling on this one and that one. It may be dark over there, but you are going to have sun. Locusts may be eating up everyone else's stuff, but you are going to have rain fall on your crops, because you are under the protection of God. "He who dwells in the secret place of the Most High shall abide under the shadow of the Almighty.... A thousand may fall at your side, and ten thousand at your right hand; but it shall not come near you" (Ps. 91:1, 7), because you walk by faith. You don't walk by what you see.

Put your trust in God. Have faith in God where you can say to your mountain, "Be thou removed and cast into the sea," and if you do not doubt in your heart, but believe that whatever you say will come to pass, you will have whatever you say.

In this book I am going to teach you how to speak to mountains and whatever stands in your way. You will learn how to say, "Be removed!" Your faith in a big God is the key to this. If you speak in faith, your faith can move mountains. When stuff gets in your way, speak to it. There is no government program that can move your mountain and no such thing as removemymountain .com. No! You speak. You learn how to walk and live by faith. Don't get depressed and caught up into financial mountains and other problems that can weigh you down. You have the power to move mountains.

God always sits on the throne. Salvation is not only about going to heaven, but it's also about ruling and reigning in your authority on earth. It's about living in the kingdom of God. We are living in the age of the kingdom now—the age of salvation, deliverance, grace, glory, power, and prosperity. Your faith is the key to bringing it all to pass.

Faith Declarations

Because of Christ I am free, and whom the Son sets free is free indeed.

I do not put my trust in man. I do not put my trust in flesh. I put my trust in God.

I live by faith. I walk by faith and not by sight.

I am responsible for my decisions and my choices. I make a decision. I choose life. I choose blessings. I choose the Word of God. I choose wisdom.

I thank You, Lord, that I am responsible for making my own way prosperous and having good success.

I have faith to speak to mountains, and they will obey me.

My heart will never depart from You, Lord. I will always serve God.

Thank You, Lord, for prosperity. I will flourish because I live in the days of the Messiah.

I will have prosperity and good success because of God's grace, in Jesus's name.

Prayers That Demolish Mountains[*]

I speak to every mountain in my life and command it to be removed and cast into the sea (Mark 11:23).

I speak to every financial mountain to be removed from my life in the name of Jesus.

Let every evil mountain hear the voice of the Lord and be removed (Mic. 6:2).

I prophesy to the mountains and command them to hear the Word of the Lord and be removed (Ezek. 36:4).

Let the mountains tremble at the presence of God (Hab. 3:10).

I contend with every mountain and command them to hear my voice (Mic. 6:1).

Lay the mountain of Esau (the flesh) to waste (Mal. 1:3).

Put forth Your hand, O Lord, and overturn the mountains by the roots (Job 28:9).

I speak to every mountain of debt to be removed and cast into the sea. Lord, You are against every destroying mountain (Jer. 51:25).

Let the mountains melt at Your presence, O God (Judg. 5:5, KJV).

---

[*] From John Eckhardt, *Prayers That Rout Demons* (Lake Mary, FL: Charisma House, 2008), 43.

Make waste the evil mountains in my life, O Lord (Isa. 42:15).

I thresh every mountain, I beat them small, and I make the hills as chaff (Isa. 41:15).

Every mountain in my way will become a plain (Zech. 4:7).

CHAPTER 1

THE PRAYER OF FAITH

And the prayer of faith will save the sick,
and the Lord will raise him up. And if he
has committed sins, he will be forgiven.

—JAMES 5:15

And whatever things you ask in prayer,
believing, you will receive.

—MATTHEW 21:22

Without faith it is impossible to please Him,
for he who comes to God must believe that
He is, and that He is a rewarder of those
who diligently seek Him.

—HEBREWS 11:6

THE PRAYER OF faith is bold and prayed from a sure
foundation of faith. The person praying this prayer is
assured of God's will for the situation or issue at hand.
They are confident and hopeful, knowing that it is God's

will to answer their prayer. "The prayer of faith has power. The prayer of faith has trust. The prayer of faith has healing for body and soul."[1]

The New Testament church was in the midst of this kind of prayer when they were praying for Peter. Right in the middle of their prayer they heard a knock on the door, and there was Peter. They were in awe. Many other examples of this prayer can be seen throughout the ministries of Jesus, the apostles, and in our lives today. The apostles prayed knowing what the will of God was for the situations they faced.

Many believers fear that when we leave things to the "will of God," somehow the solution, provision, healing, or deliverance they need will not be given. But they don't know the will of God for them. According to the model prayer that Jesus gave His disciples in Matthew 6:9–11, we are to pray for God's will to be done. But people "resign their intelligence at that point to the unknown God....It does not say, 'If it be thy will' and stop there. There is a comma there, not a period. The prayer is this, 'Thy will be done, as in heaven, so in earth' (Luke 11:2)."[2] I'd say that is a significant difference.

FAITH IN GOD'S WILL

When we pray the prayer of faith, we are praying God's will for how things are in heaven to be done in the earth realm. Here is where a clear revelation of the kingdom is very important. Is there sickness in heaven? Is there lack in heaven? Are there any unsaved in heaven? We must have faith to believe that God wants His will for our health, prosperity, and full salvation to be manifested not only when we go to heaven but even as we dwell on earth. It's for His glory. When people see that God's people have His ear and He is answering their prayers, that is a testimony for Him. People are drawn to God when they can see through His witnesses that He is a God who hears, and if He hears, they know He will answer.

Jesus said, "I have come that they may have life, and that they may have it more abundantly" (John 10:10). You have to gain the assurance that is God's will for you, so when you pray, you will pray with confidence and faith that He will answer you.

> The Lord wants us to have more faith. When several are praying together for the same petition and one has prayed the prayer of faith, the Holy Ghost will glorify Jesus by witnessing the prayer that is heard....The Lord wants us to know that He has heard us. We need to thank and praise Him for answering and that will help us a great deal when we pray.[3]
>
> —WILLIAM SEYMOUR

WONDER-WORKING FAITH

There are many different kinds of faith: (1) faith that gets you saved, (2) general faith in whatever appears real to you, (3) faith that God is real, (4) faith that your chair won't break when you sit in it, and so on. But what I am talking about in this chapter is another kind of faith—a special faith. The Amplified Bible reads, "To another [wonder-working] faith by the same [Holy] Spirit" (1 Cor. 12:9). This faith, also called special faith, is one of the spiritual gifts. Smith Wigglesworth said that you often find that if you will make a step of faith and use your own faith that you as an individual Christian have, when you come to the end of that faith, very often this supernatural faith will take over. The reason it hasn't happened with a lot of folks is that they don't first use what they already have.

> Every believer already has general faith or saving faith, which is also a gift. Ephesians 2:8 says, "For by grace are ye saved through faith; and that not of yourselves: it is the gift of God."
>
> The faith that you are saved by is a gift of God, but it is not one of the nine gifts of the Spirit. Saving faith is given to you through hearing the Word, because the Bible says, "So then faith [saving faith] cometh by hearing, and hearing by the word of God" (Rom. 10:17).
>
> The faith we are talking about—"special faith"—is something other than general faith or saving faith. It is a supernatural manifestation of the Holy Spirit whereby a believer is empowered with special faith, or wonder-working faith, and it is beyond simple saving faith.[4]

This is the kind of faith that you need to be able to move the obstructions and obstacles in your way.

Sickness, financial strife, abuse, pride, unemployment, bondages, and strongholds of all kinds will not be able to stay in your life when you pray with wonder-working faith. They must go!

All you have to do is believe, and nothing will be impossible for you (Mark 9:23). That is special. Special faith will cause you to speak to stubborn demons and say, "I command you, come out of him and enter him no more!" (v. 25). Special faith is the miracle-working faith that Jesus had during His ministry on the earth, and He said that we would walk in even greater power and perform greater things than He did.

PROPHESY TO YOUR MOUNTAIN

I am reminded of the passage in Ezekiel where God instructed the prophet to prophesy to a valley of dry bones. While Ezekiel had no comparison in the natural that what God was asking him to do was possible, he had an unshakable faith in the God who commanded him.

> And He said to me, "Son of man, can these bones live?" So I answered, "O Lord GOD, You know." Again He said to me, "Prophesy to these bones, and say to them, '*O dry bones, hear the word of the Lord*!'...So I prophesied as I was commanded; and as I prophesied, there was a noise, and suddenly a rattling; and the bones came together, bone to bone. Indeed, as I looked, the sinews and the flesh came upon them, and the skin covered them over...and breath came into

them, and they lived, and stood upon their feet,
an exceedingly great army.

—EZEKIEL 37:3–10, EMPHASIS ADDED

Can your mountain hear you prophesying to it the Word of the Lord? I challenge you to begin to incorporate the prayer of faith and begin to prophesy to your mountain. Say to it, "Mountain, the Word says that if I believe, nothing will be impossible to me. Mountain, I believe the Word of the Lord. And the Word of the Lord to you today is BE THOU REMOVED and cast into the sea!"

Even if you have never seen deliverance, healing, or breakthrough in your life or family before, know that today is a new day and that your faith in the power of God will make the impossible possible for you.

PRAYERS THAT RELEASE SPECIAL FAITH*

I declare that I, like Enoch, have a testimony that I please God through my faith (Heb. 11:5).

Because of my faith I am pleasing to God, and He will reward me because I seek after Him diligently (Heb. 11:6).

By faith I will sojourn in the land of promise, as in a strange country, dwelling in tabernacles with Isaac and Jacob, as I am an heir of the same promise (Heb. 11:9).

* Some prayers are from John Eckhardt, *Prayers That Bring Healing* (Lake Mary, FL: Charisma House, 2010), 61–63.

I will forsake any bondage that seeks to entrap me, looking forward by faith and setting my eyes on Him who is invisible (Heb. 11:27).

I decree and declare that by faith I will walk through my trials on dry ground, and my enemies will be drowned (Heb. 11:29).

I will encircle the immovable walls in my life, and by my faith those walls will fall down (Heb. 11:30).

Like Rahab, I will receive the men of God with peace. I will not perish with those who do not believe (Heb. 11:31).

I will subdue kingdoms, rain down righteousness, obtain promises, and stop the mouths of lions because of my faith (Heb. 11:33).

I declare that I will not only receive a good testimony of faithfulness, but I will also receive all that God has promised (Heb. 11:39–40).

I am established and anointed by God (2 Cor. 1:21).

I activate my mustard seed of faith and say to this mountain of sickness and disease in my life, "Be removed and go to another place." Nothing will be impossible to me (Matt. 17:20).

Because You have anointed me, I have faith and do not doubt that I can speak to any illness, curse it at the root, and cause it to dry up and die, just as You did to the fig tree. I also know that if I tell to this mountain of sickness that is in my way to move and be cast into the sea, it shall be done (Matt. 21:21).

I declare that I have uncommon, great faith in the power of Jesus Christ, faith that cannot be found anywhere else (Matt. 8:10).

Just as Jesus stood in the boat and spoke to the storm, I too can stand in the midst of the storms in my life and rebuke the winds and the waves to command calmness in my life. My faith overrides all my fears (Matt. 8:26).

I will not sink into faithlessness and doubt; I will be upheld by the mighty hand of God (Matt. 14:31).

I pray as Your anointed disciples prayed, "Increase my faith!" (Luke 17:5).

I will not be weak in faith. Like Abraham, I declare that my body is not dead but alive to birth out the gifts and anointing God has set aside for me (Rom. 4:19).

I will not stagger at the promise of God through unbelief, but I will stand strong in the faith, giving glory to God (Rom. 4:20).

My faith increases the more I hear, and hear by the Word of God (Rom. 10:17).

Even though I go through many common trials in this life, God, I declare that You are faithful. You will not allow me to face things beyond what I can stand. You have ordered a way of escape for me, and through Your strength I can bear it (1 Cor. 10:13).

I walk by faith and not by sight (2 Cor. 5:7).

I declare that I feel the substance and see the evidence of the things that I have faith for (Heb. 11:1).

You are Lord of all, and the worlds were framed by Your very words. You spoke into existence unseen things (Heb. 11:3).

I see through the eyes of faith the promise of things afar off. I am persuaded of their reality. I embrace them, knowing that I am a stranger and pilgrim on this earth (Heb. 11:13).

I will stand firm and not waver. I will come boldly before God, asking in faith (James 1:6).

I will not suffer shipwreck in my life, because I have faith and a good conscience (1 Tim. 1:19).

I thank You, God, that the testing of my faith produces patience to wait for Your Word to manifest in my life (James 1:3).

I hold the mystery of faith with a pure conscience (1 Tim. 3:9).

I declare that my faith works together with my works, and by my works my faith is made perfect (James 2:22).

I will show my faith by the works I do (James 2:18).

I am blessed with believing Abraham because I am a person of faith (Gal. 3:9).

By faith the walls built up around the territory God has promised to me will fall like the walls of Jericho (Heb. 11:30).

Because of my faith in Jesus I have boldness and confident access to approach God (Eph. 3:12).

I am a son of Abraham because I have faith (Gal. 3:7).

I am a son of God because I have faith in Christ Jesus (Gal. 3:26).

I go in peace because my faith has saved me (Luke 7:50).

My faith is alive (James 2:17).

The Spirit of God has given me the gift of faith (1 Cor. 12:9).

I have faith in God (Mark 11:22).

Let it be to me according to my faith (Matt. 9:29).

No man has dominion over my faith. I stand by faith (2 Cor. 1:24).

Like Stephen, I do great wonders and signs because I am full of faith (Acts 6:8).

I will arise and go my way, because my faith has made me well (Luke 17:19).

I receive my sight; my faith has made me well (Luke 18:42).

My faith is not in the wisdom of men but in the power of God (1 Cor. 2:5).

I will not be sluggish. I will imitate those who through faith and patience inherit the promises of God (Heb. 6:12).

The just shall live by faith (Rom. 1:17).

The righteousness of God is revealed to me through faith in Jesus (Rom. 3:22).

I am justified by my faith in Jesus (Rom. 3:26).

I have access by faith to the grace of God (Rom. 5:2).

I am raised to life through faith in Christ (Col. 2:12).

I do not fear the wrath of the king, and by faith I forsake Egypt (Heb. 11:27).

By faith I receive the promise of God in my life (Gal. 3:22).

My faith and hope are in God (1 Pet. 1:21).

My faith will not fail (Luke 22:32).

By faith the promise of God is sure to me, the seed of Abraham (Rom. 4:16).

I pray the prayer of faith and will see the sick saved and raised up (James 5:15).

I take the shield of faith and quench all the fiery darts of the wicked one (Eph. 6:16).

I put on the breastplate of faith and love (1 Thess. 5:8).

I obtain for myself good standing and great boldness in my faith in Christ Jesus (1 Tim. 3:13).

The Holy Scriptures make me wise for salvation through faith in Christ Jesus (2 Tim. 3:15).

The sharing of my faith is effective because I acknowledge that every good thing that is in me is because of Jesus (Philem. 1:6).

I am justified by my faith in Christ (Gal. 2:16).

I am rich in faith and an heir to the kingdom (James 2:5).

I contend earnestly for the faith that was delivered to me (Jude 3).

The Word profits me well because I mix what I have heard with faith (Heb. 4:2).

Like Abel, I offer an excellent sacrifice to God because of my faith (Heb. 11:4).

I please God, and He rewards me because I have faith (Heb. 11:6).

By faith I obey and go out to the place I will receive as an inheritance (Heb. 11:8).

By faith I dwell in the land of promise (Heb. 11:9).

CHAPTER 2

THE PRAYER OF THE RIGHTEOUS

The effective, fervent prayer of a righteous
man avails [accomplishes] much.
—JAMES 5:16

THE CONDITION OF the heart is a major aspect of
answered prayer. It is sincere prayer from the heart
that makes the power of God available. The Amplified
Version of James 5:16 reads, "The earnest (heartfelt, continued) prayer of a righteous man makes tremendous
power available [dynamic in its working]." James is
encouraging the believers by the example of Elijah, who
was a man subject to the same passions as any man, yet
his prayer shut up the heavens: "Elijah was a man with
a nature like ours, and he prayed earnestly that it would
not rain; and it did not rain on the land for three years
and six months. And he prayed again, and the heaven
gave rain, and the earth produced its fruit" (vv. 17–18).

Elijah was known for his fervency. *Fervent* means
having or showing great emotion or zeal, ardent,

extremely hot or glowing. Many try to divorce emotion from prayer, but God responds to those who are sincere and ardent. The implication is that those who are righteous will pray this way. This is because righteousness stirs us to pray for justice, equity, fairness, and the things that are right.

Righteous people will have a passion in prayer. When they open their mouths and begin to pray and speak to the mountains in their lives, wisdom, life, truth, and justice flow out. Their environment begins to take on the attributes of the kingdom as they speak it into existence.

Righteousness is the foundation for the kingdom of God. In order for the kingdom of God—righteousness, peace, and joy in the Holy Spirit (Rom. 14:17)—to be manifested in your life, you must be righteous. His kingdom comes and His will is done when a righteous person prays.

The Lord's eyes and ears are on the righteous. He hears their prayers and answers them. He rewards the righteous and saves them out of all their troubles. God seeks to level the mountains of the righteous. He seeks to make roads in the wilderness and rivers in the desert for the righteous. He will do this for you just as He did for Daniel:

> In those days I, Daniel, was mourning three full weeks. I ate no pleasant food, no meat or wine came into my mouth, nor did I anoint myself at all, till three whole weeks were fulfilled....Suddenly, a hand touched me...and he said to me,

"O Daniel, man greatly beloved, understand the
words that I speak to you, and stand upright, for I
have now been sent to you....Do not fear, Daniel,
for from the first day that you set your heart to
understand, and to humble yourself before your
God, your words were heard; and I have come
because of your words."

—DANIEL 10:2, 10–12

The Lord will send angelic reinforcement to help you
stand and be victorious over the evil forces that seek to
destroy God's Word over your life. Daniel prayed with
fervency and passion, and his prayer was effective—it
accomplished much! An angel of the Lord came to him,
strengthened him, and delivered a prophetic word so
powerful that it is still being activated and fulfilled for
the body of Christ today.

WHO ARE THE RIGHTEOUS?

The righteous are those who are in right standing with
God. Because of Christ we can all stand upright in the
presence of God and boldly make our requests known
to Him—if we have accepted His sacrifice. The righteous
are bold as a lion.

The righteous are those who have and occupy—or take
up residence in—the kingdom of heaven. The Bible says
that the righteous shine in the kingdom of their Father.
Light and gladness shine on their path. They may have
many afflictions, but God delivers them out of them all.

The righteous have the mind of Christ. Their thoughts are right and pure. They keep a sober mind. They do not claim or trust in their own righteousness, but they live under the imputed righteousness of Christ. They are open to the correction of the Lord and His ministers. They receive wise counsel and apply it to their lives.

The righteous are immovable and unable to be uprooted out of their place in God. Their house will stand. Their children will be saved, blessed, and have plenty to eat. They will flourish and will not be overthrown by the enemy. They will not be led astray by discouragement, doubt, or depression. The righteous are sure that God will come and save them.

The righteous are generous and merciful. They are concerned and care for the poor. They are active in areas of justice. They seek justice. They walk with integrity. Enduring riches and honor are with them. They are fruitful, and their labors lead to life.

The righteous welcome godly associations and wisdom. They know who is around them. They are careful with whom they let into their inner circle. People who associate with wickedness and ungodliness can hinder you from breaking through. Your association with them can lead you to a place of ineffectiveness in the spirit. Your words and prayers will not move mountains because your association with them has led you astray (Prov. 12:26). Sometimes you have to tell your friends and crooked business partners to go.

When you find yourself coming up against a block in the spirit, take a look around at your friends. The Bible says, "Do not be unequally yoked with unbelievers." They may even be the open door to some of the stubborn demons and strongholds you are struggling with. Be wise. Let the counsel of the ungodly be far from you (Job 22:18, AMP).

THE RIGHTEOUS AND THE COVENANT OF GOD

You are "the righteous" and can claim all the benefits of the righteous by being in covenant with God. God doesn't haphazardly bless people. He doesn't just bless people for any reason. God blesses those with whom He is in covenant. Being in covenant with God is a contract or a promise of His peace, safety, favor, protection, health, and prosperity. And God does not break His promises or go back on His Word (Num. 23:19; Isa. 55:11).

Covenant with God is a mutual blessing. God gets a people, and we get God (Lev. 26:12). We become the righteousness of God through Christ Jesus (Rom. 3:22). Because we have received the new covenant through His shed blood on the cross, His righteousness is imputed to, or counted toward, us. We become "the righteous." But if we don't remain in God and give ourselves over to Him completely, He doesn't have "a people." Then there is no need for the covenant. We cannot be God's own if we do not walk according to His covenant. He cannot claim us and put His name on us. We can pray for peace in the storm and speak to mountains all year long, but without Jesus, who is the Prince of Peace and the waymaker, peace will not come and mountains will not be removed.

The righteous possess the kingdom of God (Matt. 5:10). Are you righteous? This goes beyond being saved. Righteousness is about continually living right before God. This is not about perfection. It's about your lifestyle being that of a righteous person. A righteous person does not live a sinful lifestyle. The righteous walk at a level of holiness and integrity. They are not liars, drunkards, and whoremongers. They don't mistreat people. If you are righteous, then the words you speak over your situation will have effect. They will cause things to line up for you in the Spirit. Your covenant with God is everlasting, and you will not fall, for He has imputed His righteousness to you through His Son, Jesus.

DECLARATIONS OF THE RIGHTEOUS

I will enter through the gate of the Lord (Ps. 118:20).

I am delivered from trouble (Prov. 11:8).

My root cannot be moved (Prov. 12:3).

I choose my friends carefully and will not be led astray (Prov. 12:26).

The memory of my name will be blessed, because I am righteous (Prov. 10:7).

My labor leads to life (Prov. 10:16).

I only desire good (Prov. 11:23).

My thoughts are right (Prov. 12:5).

My house will stand, and I will not be overthrown (Prov. 12:7).

I have a refuge in death and will not be banished (Prov. 14:32).

I walk in integrity, and my children are blessed (Prov. 20:7).

I do not covet greedily. I give and spare not (Prov. 21:26).

I am bold as a lion (Prov. 28:1).

I am not snared by transgression. I sing and rejoice (Prov. 29:6).

I consider the cause of the poor (Prov. 29:7).

I cry out, and the Lord hears. He delivers me out of all my troubles (Ps. 34:17).

I show mercy and give (Ps. 37:21).

I inherit the land and dwell in it forever (Ps. 37:29).

I speak wisdom, and my tongue talks of justice (Ps. 37:30).

The gates are open to me and I enter in, because I keep the truth (Isa. 26:2).

Justice will not be taken from me (Isa. 5:23).

I will not be destroyed with the wicked (Gen. 18:23).

I will go away into eternal life (Matt. 25:46).

My words are like choice silver (Prov. 10:20).

My words encourage many (Prov. 10:21).

My hope will be gladness (Prov. 10:28).

I will never be removed (Prov. 10:30).

My words bring forth wisdom (Prov. 10:31).

I am delivered through knowledge (Prov. 11:9).

I flourish like foliage (Prov. 11:28).

My roots yield fruit (Prov. 12:12).

The light in me rejoices and will not be put out (Prov. 13:9).

When I rejoice, there is great glory (Prov. 28:12).

I will see the fall of the wicked (Prov. 29:16).

I am glad and rejoice before God. Yes, I rejoice exceedingly (Ps. 68:3).

I will never be shaken. I will be in everlasting remembrance (Ps. 112:6).

I give thanks to Your name and dwell in Your presence (Ps. 140:13).

I will flourish like a palm tree. I will grow like a cedar in Lebanon (Ps. 92:12).

I eat to the satisfying of my soul (Prov. 13:25).

I will surely live and not sin, because I take the warning (Ezek. 3:21).

I speak what is acceptable (Prov. 10:32).

My fruit is a tree of life (Prov. 11:30).

I am rewarded here on earth (Prov. 11:31).

In my house there is much treasure (Prov. 15:6).

The name of the Lord is my strong tower. I run to it and am safe (Prov. 18:10).

My salvation is from the Lord. He is my strength in the time of trouble (Ps. 37:39).

It will be well with me, because I will eat the fruit of my doings (Isa. 3:10).

I will hold my way and will grow stronger and stronger (Job 17:9).

My words are a well of life (Prov. 10:11).

My desires will be granted (Prov. 10:24).

I have an everlasting foundation (Prov. 10:25).

I come through trouble and will not be ensnared (Prov. 12:13).

I think carefully before speaking (Prov. 15:28).

I will be glad in the Lord and will trust Him (Ps. 64:10).

I will flourish and live in an abundance of peace (Ps. 72:7).

My horns will be exhalted (Ps. 75:10).

My children will be delivered (Prov. 11:21).

The scepter of wickedness will not rest on the land allotted to me (Ps. 125:3).

I will not be forsaken, nor will my children beg for bread (Ps. 37:25).

I will shine forth like the sun in the kingdom of my Father (Matt. 13:43).

I do not walk according to the flesh but according to the Spirit (Rom. 8:4).

The ways of the Lord are right, and I walk in them (Hosea 14:9).

I am born of God, because I practice righteousness (1 John 2:29).

Riches and honor are with me, enduring riches and righteousness (Prov. 8:18).

The kingdom of heaven is mine, for I am persecuted for the sake of righteousness (Matt. 5:10).

I traverse the way of righteousness, in the midst of the paths of justice (Prov. 8:20).

The Lord loves me because I follow righteousness (Prov. 15:9).

PRAYERS OF THE RIGHTEOUS

Lord, do not allow my soul to famish, and do not cast away my desire (Prov. 10:3).

Lord, I cast my burden on You, and You will sustain me. You will not permit me to be moved (Ps. 55:22).

Lord, You have discerned that I am righteous and one who serves You. Make me Your jewel (Mal. 3:17–18).

Lord, let me be counted worthy of Your kingdom (2 Thess. 1:5).

Lord, bring my soul out of prison that I may praise Your name. Let the righteous surround me, for You will deal bountifully with me (Ps. 142:7).

Lord, let it be granted to me to be arrayed in fine linen, clean and bright (Rev. 19:8).

Lord, let the righteous requirement of the law be fulfilled in me (Rom. 8:4).

Let the wickedness of the wicked come to an end, but establish the just, for You, O God, test the heart and mind (Ps. 7:9).

Far be it from You, O Lord, to slay the righteous with the wicked. You, the Judge of all the earth, will do right (Gen. 18:25).

Hear in heaven, O Lord, and act, and judge Your servants, condemning the wicked, bringing his way on his head. Justify the righteous according to his righteousness (1 Kings 8:32).

I thank You, Lord, for the crown of righteousness that is laid up for me, for You will give it to me on that Day—and not just to me, but to all who have loved Your appearing (2 Tim. 4:8).

Let all the righteous blood shed on the earth from Abel to Zechariah come upon the heads of the scribes and Pharisees (Matt. 23:35).

Let the righteous strike me; it shall be a kindness. Let him rebuke me; it shall be as excellent oil; let my head not refuse it. For still my prayer is against the deeds of the wicked (Ps. 141:5).

Hear me when I call, O God of my righteousness (Ps. 4:1).

God is with the generation of the righteous. My enemies are in great fear (Ps. 14:5).

Because I practice righteousness, I am righteous, just as He is righteous (1 John 3:7).

Let the Lord reward me according to my righteousness, and according to the cleanliness of my hands may He reward me (2 Sam. 22:21).

Let me not trust in my own righteousness, despising others (Luke 18:9).

I hunger and thirst for righteousness. Lord, fill me (Matt. 5:6).

Lord, let me walk in the way of goodness and keep to the paths of righteousness (Prov. 2:20).

Let me not find treasures in wickedness, which profits me nothing, but let righteousness deliver me from death (Prov. 10:2).

Let blessings be upon my head (Prov. 10:6).

Let righteousness guard my way so that I will be found blameless (Prov. 13:6).

Let me be repaid with good (Prov. 13:21).

Let me not be reproached by sin but exhalted in righteousness (Prov. 14:34).

Let not my ways be an abomination unto the Lord (Prov. 15:9).

Lord, do not be far from me. Hear my prayer (Prov. 15:29).

The eyes of the Lord are on me, and His ears are open to my cry (Ps. 34:15).

Many are my afflictions, but Lord, You deliver me out of them all (Ps. 34:19).

Let light and gladness be sown for me (Ps. 97:11).

CHAPTER 3

THE PERSISTENT PRAYER

> Keep on asking, and you will receive what
> you ask for. Keep on seeking, and you will
> find. Keep on knocking, and the door will
> be opened to you.
>
> —MATTHEW 7:7, NLT

SOMETIMES ONCE ISN'T enough, and one prayer hasn't said it all or broken through. You find yourself praying again and again until you see the lines in the spirit begin to line up in your favor. This is called the persistent prayer. Persistence is another aspect of answered prayer. Persistence means not giving up. Persistence shows an earnest desire to receive an answer. This again reveals the condition of the heart. People who are not persistent lack the intensity that should be in the heart of righteous people.

Webster's Dictionary defines *persist* this way:

1. To go on resolutely or stubbornly in spite of opposition, importunity, or warning

2. To remain unchanged or fixed in a specified character, condition, or position

3. To be insistent in the repetition or pressing of an utterance (as a question or an opinion)

4. To continue to exist especially past a usual, expected, or normal time[1]

Synonyms for *persist* include to carry on, dig in, hang on, keep up, follow through with, knuckle down, abide, endure, hold on, hold up, last, remain, linger, stay, stick around, tarry, carry through, and prevail.[2] Persistence reveals an earnest desire to receive. Earnest means showing deep sincerity or seriousness, determined. Godly determination will be the force that drives people to pray without ceasing and be steadfast until the answer comes.

Does this sound like your prayer life? I know of many believers who get weary in prayer. They pray for a little while and get discouraged because the answer didn't come. The enemy never ceases to make war with the saints. He will never give up because His time is short. You must never cease praying.

The definition of *persist* also mirrors godly attributes. God persists and continues with us in our humanity. Jesus never ceases to make intercession for us (Isa. 53:12; Rom. 8:34). God is faithful. He sticks with us. He carries us through. When we pray persistent prayers, we are praying in the character of God.

THE CONTINUING PRAYER

Persist also means to continue past a usual or expected time. In the Bible there are many references to continuing prayer. This is also a prayer of persistence, of not giving up. Hannah is an example of one who continued in prayer to the point that the priest Eli thought she was drunk (1 Sam. 1:12–13). Hannah persisted until she got an answer—her son Samuel. In Acts 1 and 2 and throughout the forming of the early church the phrases "continued in prayer," "continued in prayer and supplication," "continued in faith, love, and holiness" are used to describe the apostles, who turned the world upside down with the gospel.

People who came to Jesus and continued with Him for days, coming before Him with their requests, were blessed, healed, delivered, and set free. Jesus had compassion on the multitude who had "continued" with Him for three days without food:

> Now Jesus called His disciples to Himself and said, "I have compassion on the multitude, because they have now continued with Me three days and have nothing to eat. And I do not want to send them away hungry, lest they faint on the way."
>
> —MATTHEW 15:32

Jesus was so moved by the people's hunger for spiritual food that He miraculously provided physical food for their bodies. They were seeking the things of the kingdom, and Jesus added the "all these things." Their persistence in seeking the Savior gave them the physical things they needed, and they weren't even praying for food.

In the verses before this creative miracle a Gentile woman came begging Jesus to deliver her demon-possessed daughter. Jesus did not answer her right away, but she persisted, even past the point of His seeming rudeness. She went even deeper with her request and bowed down in worship before Him. She was not giving up. She was willing to take even the crumbs from His table. She was willing, like the woman with the issue of blood, to just have a fragment of His healing virtue. She knew there was miracle power even in the leftovers of Jesus's presence. Jesus was amazed by her faith:

> "O woman, great is your faith! Let it be to you as you desire." And her daughter was healed from that very hour.
>
> —MATTHEW 15:28

Another example of persistence is found in Luke 18:35–40:

> Then it happened, as He was coming near Jericho, that a certain blind man sat by the road begging. And hearing a multitude passing by, he asked what it meant. So they told him that Jesus of Nazareth was passing by. And he cried out, saying, "Jesus, Son of David, have mercy on me!" Then those who went before warned him that he should be

quiet; but he cried out all the more, "Son of David, have mercy on me!" So Jesus stood still and commanded him to be brought to Him.

The people told this man to be quiet, don't bother Jesus. But this man was desperate. He was insistent on being heard so that Jesus could minister to him. His persistence resulted in his sight being restored.

James 5:11 says, "Behold, we count them happy which endure [continue, press, persist]. Ye have heard of the patience of Job, and have seen the end of the Lord; that the Lord is very pitiful, and of tender mercy" (KJV).

Some believers feel that we should not have to beg God to do anything for us. "If it's His will," many have said, "then He will just do it. We just need to believe." There may be times when this is true, but the people in the Bible who wanted a touch from Jesus did everything wrong according to the way the church people thought it needed to be done. They were loud. They were desperate. They were inappropriate. They cried out. They bowed low. They embarrassed themselves and others. They begged. They had mountains that needed to be moved, and they didn't care what was in the way of getting to Jesus. They just knew He was the One with the answer, and they did not give up asking and crying out to Him until they had their breakthrough.

PRAYING THROUGH

Believers who've been around for a while know this kind of persistence in prayer as tarrying or praying through. Smith Wigglesworth says:

> We ought not to stop until we pray through and receive our requests from God. We should prevail with God until we get a witness. Elijah prayed for rain and sent his servant seven times until he got the witness, which was a cloud the size of a man's hand. Then Elijah arose and went to tell Ahab that the rain was coming (1 Kings 18:42–44).
>
> Paul prayed thrice for a certain thing before God answered him (2 Cor. 12:8). God heard the first time, but Paul did not get the answer until he prayed three times.
>
> Oh, we should press or claim before the throne until we receive witness by the power of the Holy Ghost. God will do just what He promises.[3]

Some of the mountains in your life are so stubborn that they require you to PUSH—pray until something happens. Do not be discouraged. Press in. Remain. Endure. Hold on. Last. The Lord hears your prayers. Don't stop praying. Your breakthrough is near. Praying consistent, earnest prayers is part of the life of a believer who is doing something right. Continue in your position of prayer despite all apparent opposition. The enemy is only on the heels of those who recognize their strength and potential in God. Never give up praying about that lost loved one, that job, your finances, your health, your marriage, your church or ministry...Whatever it is, God is persisting with you. He has compassion on those who continue with Him.

PERSISTENT, EARNEST PRAYERS

I continue earnestly in prayer, being vigilant in it with thanksgiving (Col. 4:2).

I beg You earnestly, O God, do not send me away (Mark 5:10).

I earnestly seek You, God, and make my supplication to You, the Almighty (Job 8:5).

I earnestly desire the best gifts (1 Cor. 12:31).

I desire earnestly to prophesy and freely speak in tongues (1 Cor. 14:39).

I earnestly seek good; therefore, I will find favor (Prov. 11:27).

I seek earnestly for God (Ps. 78:34).

I groan, earnestly desiring to be clothed with the habitation of heaven (2 Cor. 5:2).

Like a servant, earnestly desiring shade, I too earnestly seek relief from my troubles (Job 7:2).

Lord, do not return to Your place. I acknowledge my offense and seek Your face. In my affliction I earnestly seek You (Hosea 5:15).

As I earnestly serve God day and night, I hope to attain the promise (Acts 26:7).

I earnestly obey Your commands, O Lord, to love You and serve You with all my heart and soul (Deut. 11:13).

I contend earnestly for the faith that was once for all delivered to the saints (Jude 3).

Like Elijah I will pray earnestly, and the rain will be subject to my prayers (James 5:17).

Lord, I hear You earnestly exhorting my fathers to obey Your voice. I will obey (Jer. 11:7).

Lord, I pray that as You earnestly remembered Ephraim, You would earnestly remember me. Let Your heart yearn for me and have mercy on me (Jer. 31:20).

As You did for Titus, put the same earnest care in my heart (2 Cor. 8:16).

I must give more earnest heed to the things I have heard, lest I drift away (Heb. 2:1).

Let the sons of God be revealed to meet creation's earnest expectation (Rom. 8:19).

Like Jesus, I am in agony. I will pray more earnestly (Luke 22:44).

Lord Jesus, I beg You earnestly to come and lay Your hands on my child that he (or she) may be healed and live (Mark 5:23).

According to my earnest expectation and hope that in nothing I will be ashamed, but with all boldness, as always, so now also Christ will be magnified in my body, whether by life or by death (Phil. 1:20).

PRAYERS THAT CONTINUE

Lord, let my continual coming into Your presence cause You to avenge me (Luke 18:5).

Lord, I am one of those who have continued with You in Your trials (Luke 22:28).

Let brotherly love continue in my life (Heb. 13:1).

Lord, because You continue forever, You have an unchangeable priesthood (Heb. 7:24).

Like Hannah, I will continue praying before the Lord (1 Sam. 1:12).

I will begin to prosper and continue to prosper until I become very prosperous (Gen. 26:13).

I will give myself continually to prayer and to the ministry of the word (Acts 6:4).

I will rejoice in hope, be patient in tribulation, and continue steadfastly in prayer (Rom. 12:12).

I am continually in the temple praising and blessing God (Luke 24:53).

Lord, my sacrifices and burnt offerings are continually before You. Thank You, Lord, that You will not rebuke me (Ps. 50:8).

I will hope continually and will praise You yet more and more (Ps. 71:14).

You are continually with me, Lord. You hold me by my right hand (Ps. 73:23).

I will keep Your law continually, forever and ever (Ps. 119:44).

Like Daniel, I will continue in prayer and service (Dan. 1:21).

I will continue in faith, love, and holiness, with self-control (1 Tim. 2:15).

I will take heed to myself and to the doctrine. I will continue in them so that I may be saved (1 Tim. 4:16).

With the assembly I will continue to worship and sing until the burnt offerings are finished (2 Chron. 29:28).

I will wait on God continually. I will return and observe mercy and justice (Hosea 12:6).

I will continue in all the things that I have learned and been assured of, knowing from whom I have learned them (2 Tim. 3:14).

I will continue with one accord in prayer and supplication (Acts 1:14).

I will continue steadfastly in the apostles' doctrine and fellowship, in the breaking of bread, and in prayers (Acts 2:42).

With purpose of heart I will continue with the Lord (Acts 11:23).

Like Peter I will continue knocking until the door is opened (Acts 12:16).

Let the truth of the gospel continue with me (Gal. 2:5).

Let the flood waters recede continually from me. Let the flood waters decrease (Gen. 8:3).

I will continue in my work on the wall (Neh. 5:16).

Eternal life is granted to me, for by patient continuance in doing good, I seek for glory, honor, and immortality (Rom. 2:7).

Lord, have compassion on me as You did for the multitudes who continued with You and had nothing to eat (Mark 8:2).

I will remain and continue in the process and joy of faith (Phil. 1:25).

I will bless the Lord at all times; His praise shall continually be in my mouth (Ps. 34:1).

Continue, O God, Your lovingkindness to those who know You, and Your righteousness to the upright in heart (Ps. 36:10).

Hold me up, and I shall be safe, and I shall observe Your statutes continually (Ps. 119:117).

I will be blessed in what I do, because I look into the perfect law of liberty and continue in it. I am not a forgetful hearer but a doer of the work (James 1:25).

I am like a widow, left alone, but I trust in God and continue in supplications and prayers both night and day (1 Tim. 5:5).

Lord, I will continue in Your covenant with me. Do not disregard me as You did with the children of Israel whom You led by the hand out of the land of Egypt (Heb. 8:9).

I will continually offer the sacrifice of praise to God and the fruit of my lips, giving praise to His name (Heb. 13:15).

CHAPTER 4

THE PRAYER OF A CONTRITE HEART

The LORD is near to those who have a broken heart, and saves such as have a contrite spirit.

—PSALM 34:18

A BROKEN SPIRIT AND a contrite heart reveal repentance and godly sorrow. This again reveals the condition of the heart. Contrite means repentant, sorrowful, and regretful. God does not despise those who are contrite and broken; His compassion is revealed toward them. God's mercy is released on the behalf of the contrite. There are many prayers in the Bible asking for the mercy of God. God responds to the cries of those who are broken and asking for mercy. Healing, deliverance, and restoration are all the result of God's mercy. Praying for mercy is a powerful way to break through. The person requesting mercy is entirely dependent upon God.

For thus says the High and Lofty One who inhabits eternity, whose name is Holy: "I dwell in the high and holy place, with him who has a contrite and humble spirit, to revive the spirit of the humble, and to revive the heart of the contrite ones."

—ISAIAH 57:15

The Lord dwells with those who have a contrite or repentant heart. He hears their prayers and grants them grace because they are sorrowful and humble.

COMING AGAINST A PRIDEFUL SPIRIT— LEVIATHAN, KING OF PRIDE

Canst thou draw out leviathan with a hook? or his tongue with a cord which thou lettest down?...His scales are his pride, shut up together as with a close seal. One is so near to another, that no air can come between them....He beholdeth all high things: he is a king over all the children of pride.

—JOB 41:1, 15–16, 34, KJV

Leviathan is the personification of the spirit of pride. Pride is the opposite of the contrite, humble, and broken heart that God dwells with. God resists pride and turns His back on those who have given pride a place of authority in their lives. Those involved in the deliverance ministry will be familiar with Leviathan, the spirit of pride. You may be surprised when you encounter spirits that identify themselves as Leviathan. I am going to break down the character of this spirit so that you can get victory over it. This may be your mountain, or this may be why a mountain in your life has not been moved.

Leviathan's scales are his pride. No air can come between them. *Air* represents *spirit*, and one of the manifestations of pride is the inability to flow in the Spirit.

Leviathan will attempt to block the flow and manifestations of the Holy Spirit in the assembly. Proud people can hinder the flow of the Spirit. Humility is a key to operating in the power of the Holy Spirit. You need the power of the Holy Spirit to be able to break through the mountainous issues of life.

Leviathan protects himself with armor. Proud people have a way of closing themselves off and hiding behind the scales of pride. When attacking Leviathan, we attack and strip his scales.

> Will he make many supplications unto thee? will
> he speak soft words unto thee?
>
> —JOB 41:3, KJV

Supplication is prayer, and Leviathan does not make supplication because he is too proud. Leviathan will therefore attempt to block prayer and attack prayer ministries. We have also dealt with people who get sleepy when praying and found that it can be connected to Leviathan. This is why the spirit of pride must be broken down when you are facing tough circumstances in life. If you are not able to be persistent in your prayers or you don't have a desire to pray, you will not break through.

Leviathan does not speak soft words. Harsh words are another sign of Leviathan. He speaks roughly and does not speak with kindness.

> Will he make a covenant with thee? Wilt thou take him as a servant for ever?
>
> —JOB 41:4, KJV

Leviathan does not keep covenant. Leviathan is a covenant-breaking spirit. Many marriages have suffered because of the operation of Leviathan. A marriage will not survive if mates operate in pride and lack submission to one another. If you are facing impossible issues in your marriage, pride may be why. Covenant is also the key way through which believers receive the blessing and peace of God in their lives. Without covenant with God, there is no peace, prosperity, protection, and healing.

Leviathan does not serve. Pride will prevent us from serving one another. Serving is an act of humility, and Leviathan hates it.

> Wilt thou play with him as with a bird? or wilt thou bind him for thy maidens?
>
> —JOB 41:5, KJV

Don't play with pride. He is not a pet.

> Lay thine hand upon him, remember the battle, do no more.
>
> —JOB 41:8, KJV

The battle with pride may be one of the most difficult you will encounter. Pride is very strong in the lives of many, and it will take a fierce determination and persistence to defeat it.

> In his neck remaineth strength…
>
> —JOB 41:22, KJV

Leviathan is stiff-necked. Stubbornness and rebellion are signs of Leviathan. Israel was always called a stiff-necked people. God judged them for their stubbornness and rebellion.

> His heart is as firm as a stone; yea, as hard as a piece of the nether millstone.
>
> —JOB 41:24, KJV

Hardness of heart is another characteristic of Leviathan. It is also a root cause of divorce. (See Matthew 19:8.) Hardness of heart is connected to unbelief and the inability to understand and comprehend spiritual things.

> He maketh the deep to boil like a pot: he maketh the sea like a pot of ointment.
>
> —JOB 41:31, KJV

Leviathan dwells in the deep. Pride can be so deeply rooted in our lives and can be difficult to pull out. He is in the sea, which represents the nations. He causes the deep to boil and is responsible for restlessness.

Thou brakest the heads of leviathan in pieces, and gavest him to be meat to the people inhabiting the wilderness.

—Psalm 74:14, kjv

God has the power to smite and break Leviathan's head (authority). God is our King working salvation (deliverance) in the earth.

I humbled my soul with fasting...

—Psalm 35:13, kjv

Fasting is a great weapon against pride. When we fast, we humble our souls. We will talk more about the power combination of prayer and fasting in the last chapter.

Deliverance from Leviathan brings peace, favor, joy, and liberty. Pharaoh was a leviathan. God released His people from Pharaoh's grip through terrible judgments. The people left Egypt and journeyed to the Promised Land, a land flowing with milk and honey. Prosperity will come with deliverance from Leviathan.

Spirits of pride include arrogance, haughtiness, puffed up, self-exaltation, vanity, rebellion, stubbornness, scorning, defiance, anti-submissive, ego, perfection, Rahab, and Orion. Pride brings destruction. Pride brings a curse and causes a person to err (Ps. 119:21). God resists the proud (James 4:6). The fear of the Lord is to hate pride and arrogance (Prov. 8:13). God attempts to hide pride from man through dreams (Job 33:14–17).

Sometimes sickness is the result of pride (vv. 17–26). Those who walk in pride, God is able to abase (Dan. 4:37).

DELIVERANCE THROUGH REPENTANCE

Pride causes rebellion and lack of repentance. Repentance shows humility and an openness to God's will being done. It shows a realization of His divine sovereignty and wisdom. Repentance is also a sign that the purpose and benefit of Christ's death have been received. When we repent, we take on the righteousness of Christ.

Sometimes the mountains of life are in your way because of unrepentant sin. You can have all the faith you want, worship and seek after God, but if you are not repenting and turning away from the sinful habits in your life, you could be making your way hard (Prov. 13:15). The good news is that if you confess your sin, God is faithful and just to forgive you of your sin and cleanse you from all unrighteousness (1 John 1:9).

Being able to speak to a mountain and have it move means that you are in right standing with God. The Bible says that the prayers of the righteous are powerful and effective (James 5:16). When you stand righteous and humble before God, believing in faith that He has heard you, you can have confidence that you will have what you have prayed.

PRAYERS FOR MERCY

Hear me when I call, O God of my righteousness: You enlarged me when I was in distress; have mercy on me, and hear my prayer (Ps. 4:1, KJV).

Have mercy upon me, O Lord; for I am weak: O Lord, heal me; for my bones are troubled (Ps. 6:2).

Have mercy upon me, O Lord; consider my trouble that I suffer from those who hate me. Lift me up from the gates of death (Ps. 9:13).

Hear, O Lord, when I cry with my voice: have mercy also upon me, and answer me (Ps. 27:7).

Hear, O Lord, and have mercy on me: Lord, be my helper (Ps. 30:10).

Have mercy on me, O Lord, for I am in trouble: my eye is consumed with grief, yes, my soul and my body (Ps. 31:9).

Have mercy on me, O God, according to Your loving-kindness: according to the multitude of Your tender mercies blot out my transgressions (Ps. 51:1).

Behold, as the eyes of servants look to the hand of their masters, and as the eyes of a maiden to the hand of her mistress; so my eyes wait on the Lord my God, until He has mercy on me (Ps. 123:2).

Jesus, Master, have mercy on me (Luke 17:13).

Jesus, son of David, have mercy on me (Luke 18:38).

I will not hold my peace, but I cry out to You all the more, "Son of David, have mercy on me" (Luke 18:39).

PRAYERS OF REPENTANCE

Lord, I repent in dust and ashes (Job 42:6).

I will repent so that I won't perish (Luke 13:3).

I repent for my wickedness and pray that the thoughts of my heart be forgiven me (Acts 8:22).

I will not tolerate the spirit of Jezebel in my life. I will not suffer anguish because of her adultery. I will repent and hold fast to what I have (Rev. 2:20–25).

Thank You, Lord, that my sins have been blotted out and times of refreshing have come from Your presence, because I have repented and been converted (Acts 3:19).

Lord, I repent. Do not remove my lampstand from its place (Rev. 2:5).

I receive the gift of the Holy Spirit, because I have repented and have been baptized (Acts 2:38).

Lord, I repent, for Your kingdom is at hand (Matt. 3:2).

Lord, I repent, that Your mighty works will be done in me (Matt. 11:20).

I will be zealous and repent because You love me and chasten me (Rev. 3:19).

I will turn to God and do the works befitting repentance (Acts 26:20).

I repent now for You will not always overlook my ignorance (Acts 17:30).

The Assyrian will not be my king, because I willingly repent (Hosea 11:5).

I repent and believe in the gospel (Mark 1:1).

I repent now of my evil way and evil doings that I may dwell in the land that the Lord has given to me and my fathers forever (Jer. 25:5).

I repent, Lord, and turn away from my idols and all my abominations (Ezek. 14:6).

Do not judge me, O Lord. I repent and turn from all my transgressions so that iniquity will not be my ruin (Ezek. 18:30).

I repent and make supplication to You, Lord, saying, "I have sinned and done wrong. I have committed wickedness" (1 Kings 8:47).

I remember what I have received and heard. I hold fast, repent, and remain watchful (Rev. 3:3).

Let repentance and remission of sins be preached in His name to all nations (Luke 24:47).

I repent before God and remain faithful toward my Lord Jesus Christ (Acts 20:21).

Godly sorrow produces repentance leading to salvation. I will not regret it (2 Cor. 7:10).

The Lord gives repentance to Israel and forgiveness of sins (Acts 5:31).

I will arise and go to my Father, and I will say to Him, "Father, I have sinned against heaven and before You" (Luke 15:18).

PRAYERS AND DECLARATIONS OF THE HUMBLE

Lord, I am humble. Guide me in justice and teach me Your ways (Ps. 25:9).

I will humble myself in the sight of the Lord, and He will lift me up (James 4:10).

I will not allow pride to enter my heart and cause me shame. I will be humble and clothed in wisdom (Prov. 11:2).

Lord, You take pleasure in me. You beautify me with salvation because I am humble (Ps. 149:4).

Lord, You will look on everyone who is proud, and You will humble them (Job 40:11).

Lord, You will save me (Ps. 18:27).

I will retain honor (Prov. 29:23).

I am better off being of a humble spirit with the lowly than dividing the spoil with the proud (Prov. 16:19).

I will humble myself under the mighty hand of God that He may exalt me in due time (1 Pet. 5:6).

My soul will make its boast in the Lord. The humble will hear of it and be glad (Ps. 34:2).

I will see what God has done and be glad. Because I seek God, my heart will live (Ps. 69:32).

I will not be like Amon, but I will humble myself before the Lord and will not trespass more and more (2 Chron. 33:23).

I will remove my turban and take off my crown and let nothing be the same. I will exalt the humble and humble the exalted (Ezek. 21:26).

I am in the midst of a meek and humble people, and they will trust in the name of the Lord (Zeph. 3:12).

I will increase my joy in the Lord. I will rejoice in the Holy One of Israel (Isa. 29:19).

Like Daniel, I will not fear, because I know that from the first day I set my heart to understand Your ways and to humble myself before You, You heard my words and have come to me (Dan. 10:12).

Lord, humble me and test me that I might do good in the end (Deut. 8:16).

I proclaim a fast right here that I might humble myself before my God, to seek from Him the right way for me and my children and all of my possessions (Ezra 8:21).

My God will humble me among His people and I will mourn for many who have sinned before and have not repented of the uncleanness, fornication, and lewdness that they have practiced (2 Cor. 12:21).

Lord, You said that if I humble myself, pray and seek Your face, and turn from my wicked ways, then You will hear from heaven and will forgive my sin and heal my land. Lord, I will do as You have commanded (2 Chron. 7:14).

Lord, You will dwell with him who has a contrite and humble spirit. You will revive the spirit of the humble and the hearts of the contrite ones. Let me be as they are (Isa. 57:15).

I will remember that the Lord my God led me all the way, even in the wilderness, to humble me and test me, to know what was in my heart, whether I would keep His commandments or not (Deut. 8:2).

God, You give more grace. You resist the proud but give grace to the humble (James 4:6).

Let me be like Moses, who was very humble, more than all the men who were on the face of the earth (Num. 12:3).

Lord, You do not forget the cry of the humble (Ps. 9:12).

Arise, O Lord! O God, lift up Your hand! Do not forget the humble (Ps. 10:12).

I will not set my mind on high things, but I will associate with the humble. I will not be wise in my own opinion (Rom. 12:16).

I will not pervert the way of the humble (Amos 2:7).

Lord, You have heard the desire of the humble; You will prepare their heart; You will cause Your ear to hear (Ps. 10:17).

I will submit myself to my elders. I will be clothed in humility, and God will give me grace (1 Pet. 5:5).

By humility and the fear of the Lord are riches, honor, and life (Prov. 22:4).

I will speak evil of no one. I will be peaceable and gentle, showing all humility to all men (Titus 3:2).

In humility I will correct those who are in opposition, and perhaps God will grant them repentance so that they may know the truth (2 Tim. 2:25).

The fear of the Lord is the instruction of wisdom, and before honor is humility (Prov. 15:33).

Before destruction the heart of a man is haughty, and before honor is humility (Prov. 18:12).

As the elect of God, holy and beloved, I will put on tender mercies, kindness, humility, meekness, and long-suffering (Col. 3:12).

I will seek the Lord. I will seek righteousness and humility so that I may be hidden in the day of the Lord's anger (Zeph. 2:3).

I take on the yoke of Christ, learning from Him, for He is meek and lowly in heart (Matt. 11:29).

I will do what the Lord requires of me: I will do justly, love mercy, and walk humbly with my God (Mic. 6:8).

I desire to be like Christ, who humbled Himself and became obedient to the point of death, even the death of the cross (Phil. 2:8).

Lord, I have humbled myself; please do not bring calamity upon me (1 Kings 21:29).

Through humility and the fear of the Lord I am given riches and honor and life (Prov. 22:4).

The Lord regards the lowly (Ps. 138:6).

I will humble myself as a little child (Matt. 18:4).

PRAYERS THAT BREAK A PRIDEFUL SPIRIT

May the Lord ruin the pride of Judah and the great pride of Jerusalem (Jer. 13:9).

I break the pride of Moab. It shall no longer be proud of its haughtiness, pride, and wrath. The lies it speaks will not be so (Isa. 16:6).

Thank You, Lord, that You turn me from my deeds and conceal my pride from me so that my soul may be kept back from the Pit and my life from perishing by the sword (Job 33:17).

Lord, I break the spirit of pride. Please answer when I cry out (Job 35:12).

I rebuke the shame that comes from a spirit of pride (Prov. 11:2).

I come against strife that comes with the spirit of pride (Prov. 13:10).

I break the spirit of pride, so that I will not fall and be destroyed (Prov. 16:18).

I break the spirit of pride. It will not bring me low. I will have a humble spirit (Prov. 29:23).

Pride will not serve as my necklace, nor will violence cover me like a garment (Ps. 73:6).

I will not be puffed up with pride and fall into the same condemnation as the devil (1 Tim. 3:6).

I break pride off of my life in the name of Jesus. I will not stumble in my iniquity like Israel, Ephraim, and Judah (Hosea 5:5).

The spirit of pride will not rule me. I shall not be desolate in the day of rebuke (Hosea 5:9).

The spirit of pride will not cause me to be scattered (Luke 1:51).

The Lord is above the spirit of the proud (Exod. 18:11).

Hear and give ear, spirit of pride. The Lord has spoken (Jer. 13:15).

The proud spirit of Ephraim and the inhabitant of Samaria will not speak (Isa. 9:9).

I command the spirit of pride to cease its persecution of the poor. Let that spirit be caught in the plots it has devised (Ps. 10:2).

Let not the foot of pride come against me, and let not the hand of the wicked drive me away (Ps. 36:11).

The Lord will cut off the pride of the Philistines (Zech. 9:6).

I break the pride of your power; I will make your heavens like iron and your earth like bronze (Lev. 26:19).

Let the pride of Moab be cut off at the root, for he is exceedingly proud of his loftiness, arrogance, pride, and the haughtiness of his heart (Jer. 48:29).

Let the pride of Israel be broken in the name of Jesus. Let them not testify to His face then go on not returning to the Lord their God (Hosea 7:10).

Lord, bring dishonor to the spirit of pride and bring into contempt all the honorable of the earth (Isa. 23:9).

I fear the Lord; therefore, I hate evil, pride, arrogance, and the evil way. I hate the perverse mouth (Prov. 8:13).

I break the spirit of the pride of life, for it is not of the Father but is of the world (1 John 2:16).

I will not be wise in my own eyes (Prov. 26:12).

Let the crown of pride, the drunkards of Ephraim, be trampled under foot (Isa. 28:3).

Like a swimmer reaches out to swim, Lord, spread out Your hands in their midst and bring down the prideful and their trickery (Isa. 25:11).

Like King Hezekiah, let prideful leaders humble themselves so that the wrath of the Lord does not come upon the people (2 Chron. 32:26).

Let not the pride of my heart deceive me. I have been brought low to the ground (Obad. 3).

Let the pride of the Jordan be brought to ruins (Zech. 11:3).

The proud in heart are an abomination to the Lord. Let them not go unpunished (Prov. 16:5)

The Lord abhors the pride of Jacob and hates his palaces. Let all their cities and everything in them be given to their enemies (Amos 6:8).

Those who walk in pride will be put down by the King of heaven (Dan. 4:37).

Those who uphold Egypt will fall; the pride of her power will come down, and those within her shall fall by the sword (Ezek. 30:6).

Let the pride of Assyria be brought down, and let the scepter of Egypt depart (Zech. 10:11).

Let those who rejoice in their pride be put to shame for any of their deeds. Let them be taken away. They shall no longer be haughty in My holy mountain (Zeph. 3:11).

I call the archers against the proud spirit of Babylon. Let all who bend the bow encamp against it all around. Let no one escape, for she has been proud against the Lord, the Holy One of Israel (Jer. 50:29).

I come against the spirit of the proud and haughty man who acts with arrogant pride (Prov. 21:24).

The Lord will bring down haughty looks (Ps. 18:27).

Let the king of Babylon be deposed from his kingly throne, for his heart is lifted up and his spirit is hardened in pride. Let his glory be taken away (Dan. 5:20).

I declare that this is the day that the Lord of hosts shall come upon everything proud and lofty, upon everything high and lifted up, and it shall be brought low (Isa. 2:12).

Let the most proud stumble and fall, and no one raise him up. Let the Lord kindle a fire in his cities, and it will devour all around him (Jer. 50:32).

I will let another man praise me, and not my own mouth; a stranger, and not my own lips (Prov. 27:2).

I dare not class myself or compare myself with those who commend themselves. They are not wise (2 Cor. 10:12).

I do not respect the proud or those who turn aside to lies. I make the Lord my trust (Ps. 40:4).

Lord, my heart is not haughty (Ps. 131:1).

Let the Lord halt the arrogance of the proud and lay low the haughtiness of the terrible (Isa. 13:11).

The Lord will not endure a haughty look and a proud heart (Ps. 101:5).

I will not talk proudly and will let no arrogance come from my mouth (1 Sam. 2:3).

The Lord resists the proud. Let me be like the humble one who receives grace from God (James 4:6).

The Lord will rise up a foreign army against the pride of the prince of Tyre. The most terrible of nations will draw their sword against the beauty of his wisdom. The Lord will defile the splendor of the proud spirit of the prince of Tyre, for his heart is lifted up declaring that he is a god. He will throw him in a pit, and he shall die the death of the slain. The Lord will break the spirit of the prince of Tyre, and he will no longer call himself a god, but a man, for he will die an outcast (Ezek. 28:2, 7–8).

I will not think of myself more highly than I ought to think. But I will remain sober minded (Rom. 12:3).

Let the prideful spirit of Haman be hanged on the gallows he prepared for God's chosen people (Esther 7:10).

I dismantle the scales of pride on the back of Leviathan (Job 41:15).

Let the rod of pride be broken in the mouth of a fool (Prov. 14:3).

Let Babylon, the glory of kingdoms and the beauty of the Chaldeans' pride, be overthrown as when God overthrew Sodom and Gomorrah (Isa. 13:19).

Let the wicked be taken in their pride and for the cursing and lying that they speak (Ps. 59:12).

The proud will not be blessed, and those who do wickedness will not be raised up. They will not tempt God and go free (Mal. 3:15).

I bridle my tongue so that it will not boast great things (James 3:5).

The Lord will bring down the haughty spirit (2 Sam. 22:28).

Let the proud and all who do wickedly become as stubble. Let neither root nor branch be left of them (Mal. 4:1).

I will not be broken off because of unbelief. I stand by faith. I will not be haughty, but I will fear (Rom. 11:20).

I will not boast about tomorrow, for I do not know what the day will bring forth (Prov. 27:1).

CHAPTER 5

THE PRAYER OF THE DESTITUTE

He shall regard the prayer of the destitute,
and shall not despise their prayer.

—PSALM 102:17

THE LORD HEARS the cry of His children when they are in need. It is His desire that none of us be in lack or in need. Psalm 102:17 says that He hears, looks upon, turns Himself toward, or holds in high regard the prayer of the destitute. Webster's dictionary defines *destitute* as "lacking something needed or desired; lacking possessions or resources; extreme poverty." [1] *Barnes' Notes* says *destitute* means:

> ..."naked;" then, poor, stripped of everything, impoverished, wholly destitute. It would thus be eminently applicable to the poor exiles in Babylon; it is as applicable to sinners pleading with God, and to the people of God themselves, destitute of everything like self-righteousness, and feeling that they have nothing in themselves, but

that they are wholly dependent on the mercy of God.[2]

This can also refer to a spiritual state. Matthew 5:3 talks about the poor in spirit. That was every one of us before we were saved. Some of us, even though we are saved, still have lack in our lives. But the Bible says that God hears our prayers. He will not leave us naked, hungry, and without provision. He is the waymaker. It is in His Father nature to give good gifts to His children (Matt. 7:11). The second part of Matthew 5:3 says that He will give you the kingdom of heaven! The wealth and riches of the kingdom of heaven are far beyond your wildest imaginations.

Knowing the promises of God concerning you and your situation, you need to be strengthened in your spirit to pray against the things in your life that are not in line with what God has for you. Don't be so quick to settle in your state of destitution and lack, thinking this is your "lot" in life. No! You have the power to speak and pray against the work of the enemy when it comes to the provision you need for your physical and spiritual life. God said that He will not despise your prayers. He will not look down on them with contempt. He does not condemn you. On the contrary, He will come to your aid quickly. (See Revelation 22:12.) He will provide ways for you that are beyond the means of men. He says to you:

> Ho! Everyone who thirsts, come to the waters;
> and you who have no money, come, buy and eat.

> Yes, come, buy wine and milk without money
> and without price. Why do you spend money for
> what is not bread, and your wages for what does
> not satisfy? Listen carefully to Me, and eat what
> is good, and let your soul delight itself in abun-
> dance. Incline your ear, and come to Me. Hear,
> and your soul shall live.
>
> —ISAIAH 55:1–3

He is a present help in your time of need. Your situation may seem hopeless, but God has already designed a
way of escape. Do not get lost in your trouble. "Look up
and lift up your heads, because your redemption draws
near" (Luke 21:28). Speak to those mountains and tell
them that your God will supply all your needs according
to His riches in glory.

YOU WILL NOT BE OVERCOME

Problems can overwhelm you and give you the feeling of
being swallowed up or overcome. *To be swallowed* means
to be devoured, to perish, to be drowned or buried. At
the end of this chapter I will give you prayers to reverse
this and cause your problems to be swallowed instead.
Demons are likened to serpents; all serpents are carnivo-
rous, and nearly all seize and swallow living food (Jer.
51:34, NIV). Most snakes have specialized body structures
that let them swallow things larger than their heads or
necks. Don't allow the enemy to swallow your life, your
finances, or your destiny. Rise up and pray for the Lord

to swallow, consume, devour, overwhelm, and bury your problems instead. Synonyms for *swallow* include deplete, take back, exhaust, bury, engross, get down, swallow, accept, withdraw, finish, engulf, inhume, eat up, entomb, absorb, run through, immerse, swallow up, sink, eat, consume, lay to rest, soak up, wipe out, polish off, steep, plunge, inter, use up.

God swallowed Pharaoh and the Egyptians in the Red Sea. God opened the earth and swallowed Korah, Dathan, and Abiram. He will do the same to the evil that comes against you.

> The waters returned and covered the chariots, the horsemen, and all the army of Pharaoh that came into the sea after them. Not so much as one of them remained. But the children of Israel had walked on dry ground in the midst of the sea, and the waters were a wall to them on their right hand and on their left.
>
> —EXODUS 14:28

> Who is like unto thee, O LORD, among the gods? who is like thee, glorious in holiness, fearful in praises, doing wonders? Thou stretchedst out thy right hand, the earth swallowed them.
>
> —EXODUS 15:11–12, KJV

> Mine enemies would daily swallow me up: for they be many that fight against me, O thou most High.
>
> —PSALM 56:2, KJV

Thou shalt make them as a fiery oven in the time of thine anger: the LORD shall swallow them up in his wrath, and the fire shall devour them.

—PSALM 21:9, KJV

Do not let the floodwaters engulf me or the depths swallow me up or the pit close its mouth over me.

—PSALM 69:15, NIV

THE CURSE OF LUCK AND FORTUNE

Many of us have latched on to a worldly way of speaking into our situations, saying this is good luck or that was bad luck. I am not lucky or merely fortunate. I am blessed. *Fortunate* means "favored by or involving good luck or fortune; lucky. Auspicious or favorable." It is derived from the pagan goddess Fortuna (equivalent to the Greek goddess Tyche)—the goddess of fortune and personification of luck in Roman religion. She might bring good luck or bad; she could be represented as veiled and blind, as in modern depictions of justice, and came to represent life's unpredictability and inconsistence.[3] She was also a goddess of fate. This definition of fortune takes it further: "chance, luck as a force in human affairs"; "lot, good fortune, misfortune"; "chance, fate, good luck"; or "chance, luck."

> The Wheel of Fortune, or Rota Fortunae, is a concept in medieval and ancient philosophy referring to the capricious nature of Fate. The wheel

belongs to the goddess Fortuna, who spins it at random, changing the positions of those on the wheel—some suffer great misfortune, others gain windfalls. Fortune appears on all paintings as a woman, sometimes blindfolded, "puppeteering" a wheel.[4]

Getting into the understanding of luck and fortune, we read in Isaiah 65:11–12 (AMP):

But you who forsake the Lord, who forget and ignore My holy Mount [Zion], who prepare a table for Gad [the Babylonian god of fortune] and who furnish mixed drinks for Meni [the god of destiny]—I will destine you [says the Lord] for the sword, and you shall all bow down to the slaughter, because when I called, you did not answer; when I spoke, you did not listen or obey. But you did what was evil in My eyes, and you chose that in which I did not delight.

Gad and Meni were the Pagan gods of fortune and destiny. Their names literally mean "troop" and "number." Gad is matched with Strong's H1408, but it is the same word as H1410, which means "troop." Meni is derived from *manah*, which means "to count, reckon, number, assign, tell, appoint, prepare." Isaiah 65:11 refers to the names of these two deities, Gad and Meni, but the thrust of the passage is that the Israelites had opted for polytheism ("that troop" and "that number") in defiance to their one God.[5]

We cannot be careless with what we use to describe the outcome of certain situations that occur in our lives. We can mistakenly be activating demonic deities to influence things that should be under God's authority.

When you turn your life over to God, you are not living by chance or the luck of the draw. You are living according to His divine plan. Jeremiah 29:11 says, "For I know the thoughts that I think toward you, says the LORD, thoughts of peace and not of evil, to give you a future and a hope." And the psalmist wrote in Psalm 37:23: "The steps of a good man are ordered by the LORD, and He delights in his way." Your life and the things you are going through are not spinning around randomly, and they are not out of control if you are in Christ. God is in control. Let your problems know this truth.

PRAYERS AGAINST CURSES AND BAD LUCK

I am not lucky; I am blessed.

In the name of Jesus, I rebuke all bad luck and bad fortune.

In the name of Jesus, I rebuke all gods and goddesses of fortune that would try to rule my life.

I repent and turn away from all superstition and belief in good luck.

In the name of Jesus, I rebuke and cast out all spirits of luck and good fortune.

In Jesus's name I renounce all items in my past associated with luck.

In the name of Jesus, I rebuke and cast out any demon trying to rule my destiny.

Lord, my destiny comes from You, and I will submit to Your plans and purposes for my life.

I declare that my steps are ordered by the Lord.

Lord, my future, success, and prosperity are in Your hands.

PRAYERS THAT
SWALLOW THE ENEMY

Lord, You are the God that swallows Your enemies.

You swallowed Pharaoh in the Red Sea.

You swallowed Korah in the earth because of his rebellion.

You caused the earth to swallow the flood released by the dragon (Rev. 12:16).

You prepared a great fish to swallow up Jonah (Jon. 1:17).

Stretch out Your right hand, O God, and let the enemy (spiritual) be swallowed up.

In the name of Jesus, I rebuke the swallower.

Let the mouth of the swallower be closed and bound, in the name of Jesus.

Let all poverty and lack in my life be swallowed up, in the name of Jesus.

Let all sickness and disease be swallowed up.

Let all discouragement and defeat be swallowed up.

Let all assignments of hell against my life be swallowed up.

In Jesus's name, let all curses and negative words spoken against my life be swallowed up.

Let all Pharaohs who attempt to follow me be swallowed up.

The enemy will not be able to swallow my finances, but he must vomit them up (Job 20:15).

Punish the enemy, and let everything he has swallowed come forth, in the name of Jesus (Jer. 51:44).

My destiny and purpose will not be swallowed up by the enemy.

My life is preserved; it will not be swallowed up by the enemy.

My enemies will not swallow me up.

Let all the rods of the enemy be swallowed by the rod of God.

Let every Korah that rises against my life be swallowed up.

In the name of Jesus, let every generational stronghold be swallowed up.

Let all persecution against my life be swallowed up.

Fear, be swallowed up.

Witchcraft, be swallowed up.

Worry, be swallowed up.

Anxiety, be swallowed up.

Frustration, be swallowed up.

Everything that would attempt to swallow me, be swallowed up, in the name of Jesus.

Let every attack of hell against my life be swallowed up, in the name of Jesus.

I will not allow foolish words to swallow me up (Eccles. 10:12).

The Lord will send from heaven and deliver me from anything that would swallow me up (Ps. 57:3).

The water will not overflow me. The deep and the pit will not swallow me up (Ps. 69:15).

None of my belongings will be swallowed by wicked people (Luke 20:47).

Let all wickedness against me be swallowed up as Pharaoh and his host were swallowed up in the Red Sea, or as Korah, Dathan, and Abiram were swallowed up in the earth.

I rebuke and bind every serpent that tries to swallow anything belonging to me, in the name of Jesus.

In the name of Jesus, I bind and rebuke every python and constrictor that would attempt to squeeze and swallow.

I break the jaws of the wicked and pluck the spoil out of his teeth, so that he cannot swallow.

Lord, rebuke the devourer for my sake.

Let any problems that would overwhelm me be swallowed up, in the name of Jesus.

Send forth your mercy and truth, and deliver me from anything that would attempt to swallow me up (Ps. 57:3).

Hear me, O Lord; for Your lovingkindness is good: turn to me according to the multitude of Your tender mercies (Ps. 69:16).

What time I am afraid, I will trust in You (Ps. 56:3).

Let not the robber swallow up my substance (Job 5:5).

Lord, You are a God of wonders; let the powers of hell be swallowed up (Exod. 15:11–12).

Let anything that comes to eat up my flesh fall and be consumed (Ps. 27:2).

I release the dagger against all Eglons that come to swallow up the resources of God's people (Judg. 3:16–18).

I come against any wave of the enemy that would attempt to swallow me up.

Let not the waves overwhelm me (Ps. 93:3).

Let not the floods overwhelm and drown me.

Lord, You tread upon the waves (Job 9:8).

Lord, on high You are mightier than the noise of many waters, yes, than the mighty waves of the sea (Ps. 93:4).

Let the proud waves be stayed (Job 38:11).

You are the God that swallows death in victory.

Let all spirits of death and destruction be swallowed up.

Let spirits of the deep, the pit, and the abyss be swallowed up.

Let Abaddon and Appolyon be swallowed up.

Let all assignments of death and hell against my family be swallowed up, in the name of Jesus.

I refuse to be swallowed up with sorrow, for the joy of the Lord is my strength.

Let debt be swallowed from my life.

Let oppression be swallowed from my life.

LEAP PRAYERS FOR SUDDEN INCREASE AND DRAMATIC ADVANCE*

I believe this is my appointed time to leap forward, in the name of Jesus.

It is my time to leap.

This is a new season of leaping for me.

I leap past all distractions, in the name of Jesus.

I leap past any people the enemy has set in my way to impede my progress.

Let my steps turn into leaps.

I leap over every wall erected by the enemy.

In the name of Jesus, I leap ahead of anyone or anything that has illegally jumped ahead of me.

I leap like a lion from Bashan like Dan.

I will leap over my enemies like David.

---

* These prayers are taken from Deut. 32:22; 2 Sam. 6:16; Ps. 18:29; Isa. 35:6; Luke 1:41; Luke 6:23; Acts 3:8; Acts 14:10.

I receive strength to leap out of all sickness and disease. I leap into my destiny and purpose, in the name of Jesus.

With excitement I leap into my future.

I leap from lack to abundance.

I leap from failure to success.

Let every place in my life that is lame leap for joy.

I take a leap of faith and do the impossible.

Let my finances grow by leaps and bounds.

Let my finances leap to a level I have not seen before.

Let wealth and prosperity leap upon my life, in the name of Jesus.

Let my wisdom increase by leaps and bounds.

Let my understanding increase by leaps and bounds.

Let my vision increase by leaps and bounds.

Let favor increase on my life by leaps and bounds.

Let my ministry grow by leaps and bounds.

Let my borders expand by leaps and bounds.

Let me leap and jump to the high places.

In the name of Jesus, let me catch up in any place I have fallen behind.

Let restoration come from anything stolen by the enemy from my life.

Let my revelation increase by leaps and bounds.

I will not be afraid to take a leap of faith at the word of the Lord.

I will leap upon the enemy and overwhelm him, in the name of Jesus.

I will leap and rejoice at the goodness of the Lord.

The Lord has given me leaping for sadness and joy for mourning.

I leap from a low place to a high place.

Let extra favor and blessing be added to my life, in the name of Jesus.

Let this year be a year of uncommon favor and blessing in my life.

Let me receive uncommon miracles and breakthroughs, in the name of Jesus.

Let me leap as a hart for joy.

I will leap into new places naturally and spiritually.

I will leap into new heights and levels.

I will leap above problems and setbacks, in the name of Jesus.

I will leap over all the traps and snares of the wicked one.

I break all chains and weights from my feet that would prevent me from leaping.

I lay aside every weight and burden that would prevent me from leaping.

I lay aside all doubt and unbelief that would keep me from leaping.

I leap from my past into my future.

I will not be afraid to leap forward with boldness and confidence.

I will leap for my God is with me.

My God encourages me and causes me to leap forward.

Let the kingdom advance in my city by leaps and bounds.

Let my timing and purpose be realigned this year, in the name of Jesus.

The way is opened for me, and I will leap into it.

I will join myself with other believers who are leaping forward.

Let the churches in my region leap forward.

Let our praise and worship leap to another level

Let my prayer life leap forward.

Let our preaching and teaching leap to another level.

I will leap forward in my giving.

Let my creativity leap to another level.

Let my faith take a quantum leap.

Let my love take a quantum leap.

Let my family leap forward into destiny.

Let my prophetic level take a quantum leap.

Let deliverance and healing take a quantum leap in my city, in the name of Jesus.

I will leap through fasting and prayer.

Let the blessings of the Lord overtake me and leap upon me, in the name of Jesus.

CHAPTER 6

MIDNIGHT AND MIDDAY PRAYER

Evening, and morning and at noon I will pray, and cry aloud, and He shall hear my voice.

—PSALM 55:17

PRAYING AT DIFFERENT times of the day can be a powerful way to move mountains and experience breakthroughs. I have always been a night person. I pray and study at night. Understanding the mystery of the night can cause you to see great breakthroughs in your spiritual life.

Midnight prayer is a time for spiritual warfare. This is the third watch of the night and one of the most important times to keep watch. This is a special time for divine government overruling human decrees! (See Exodus 12–14.) This is when the deep sleep falls upon men according to Acts 20:7–12. Remember, according to Matthew 13:25, while men slept, the enemy went to sow tares. This is therefore a period of heightened satanic activities. The devil operates at this time because this is the time that men are sleep and there are not so many people praying to oppose him (1 Kings 3:20; Matt. 13:25).

> Night is also a time of anguish and fear for many, when pain, guilt, fear, and despair can seem almost unendurable. Many of the psalms call out to God from the depths of distress, for mercy, help, justice, victory over evil. Praying them, we give voice to the cries of the poor and troubled, those who are unable to turn to God themselves, or who do not even believe in God. We identify with those who are suffering, and call out with them and for them. Our prayer rises to God in the hours of darkness as an act of solidarity with those experiencing the night of the cross.[1]

In Psalm 42:8 we read, "The LORD will command His lovingkindness in the daytime, and in the night His song shall be with me—a prayer to the God of my life." According to *Adam Clarke's Commentary*, this verse is saying that God will give a special commission for His loving-kindness to visit us in the night hours, that He will allow His mercy to continue in our prayers, and give us power to make the best use of this visitation.[2]

That is a powerful revelation on the mystery of the night. When we pray at night, the Lord's love, kindness, and mercy will dwell in the midst of our prayers and be available to us in their full power. So if you are experiencing intense demonic opposition, the midnight hour would be an ideal place to establish a prayer post or vigil until you experience breakthrough.

Breakthroughs at Midnight

The night has been established by covenant. Jeremiah 33:20 says, "Thus saith the LORD; If ye can break my covenant of the day, and my covenant of the night, and that there should not be day and night in their season" (KJV). Great breakthroughs can occur when we praise and pray at night. Midnight is a time when God does supernatural things. In Psalm 119:62 the psalmist said, "At midnight I will rise to give thanks unto thee because of thy righteous judgments" (KJV). Here is a list of other blessings or breakthroughs that occur at midnight.

Midnight is a time of release from every spiritual prison.

> And at *midnight* Paul and Silas prayed, and sang praises unto God: and the prisoners heard them.
> —ACTS 16:25, KJV, EMPHASIS ADDED

You can provoke God with fearful praises at midnight just as David and Paul did. It is a time of release from every spiritual prison; when you utilize the mystery of midnight prayers, it will initiate the earthquake of deliverance that would set you free.

> Then Moses said, "Thus says the LORD, 'About midnight I will go out into the midst of Egypt.'"
> —EXODUS 11:4

87

God's deliverance of Israel began at midnight.

> And it came to pass at midnight that the LORD struck all the firstborn in the land of Egypt, from the firstborn of Pharaoh who sat on his throne to the firstborn of the captive who was in the dungeon, and all the firstborn of livestock.
>
> —EXODUS 12:29

Destruction of the enemy's gate happens at midnight.

> And Samson lay low till midnight; then he arose at midnight, took hold of the doors of the gate of the city and the two gateposts, pulled them up, bar and all, put them on his shoulders, and carried them up to the top of the hill that faces Hebron.
>
> —JUDGES 16:3

The bridegroom comes at midnight.

> Now it happened at midnight that the man [Boaz] was startled, and turned himself: and there, a woman [Ruth] was lying at his feet.
>
> —RUTH 3:8

> And at midnight a cry was heard: "Behold, the bridegroom is coming; go out to meet him!"
>
> —MATTHEW 25:6

Midnight is a time to ask.

> And He said unto them, "Which of you shall have a friend, and go to him at midnight and say to him, 'Friend, lend me three loaves.'"
>
> —LUKE 11:5

Catch the thief at midnight.

> And she arose at midnight, and took my son from beside me, while thine handmaid slept, and laid it in her bosom, and laid her dead child in my bosom.
>
> —1 KINGS 3:20, KJV

> You make darkness, and it is night, in which all the beasts of the forest creep about.
>
> —PSALM 104:20

God can instruct us at night.

> I will bless the LORD who has given me counsel: my heart also instructs me in the night seasons.
>
> —PSALM 16:7

God can visit us at night.

> You have tested my heart; You have visited me in the night; You have tried me and have found nothing; I have purposed that my mouth shall not transgress.
>
> —PSALM 17:3

We can meditate on God and the Word at night.

> When I remember You on my bed, I meditate on You in the night watches.
>
> —PSALM 63:6

> My eyes are awake through the night watches, that I might meditate on Your word.
>
> —PSALM 119:148

It is good to desire God in the night.

> With my soul I have desired You in the night, yes, by my spirit within me I will seek You early; for when Your judgments are in the earth, the inhabitants of the world will learn righteousness.
>
> —ISAIAH 26:9

Nehemiah could see the desolation of the broken walls of the city at night.

> So I went up in the night by the valley, and viewed the wall; then I turned back and entered by the Valley Gate, and so returned.
>
> —NEHEMIAH 2:15

The Lord appeared to Solomon at night.

> Then the LORD appeared to Solomon by night, and said to him, "I have heard your prayer, and have chosen this place for Myself as a house of sacrifice."
>
> —2 CHRONICLES 7:12

Nicodemus sought Jesus at night.

> Nicodemus (he who came to Jesus by night, being one of them)...
>
> —JOHN 7:50

Angels of deliverance can come at night.

> But at night an angel of the Lord opened the prison doors and brought them out.
>
> —ACTS 5:19

> For there stood by me this night an angel of the God to whom I belong and whom I serve.
>
> —ACTS 27:23

DESTROYING THE WORKS OF DARKNESS

When the king of Syria came to arrest Elisha in 2 Kings 6:13–14, he came in the night. For the kingdom of darkness, nighttime is conference time. It is when the enemies meet to deliver their reports, re-strategize and take decisions concerning the fate of many—including Christians. It is also when they renew covenants, curses, and sacrifices. It is the time they supervise the burdens, punishment, and yokes already placed on their victims. But more importantly, it is the time they alter the destiny of many. Every night activity of the satanic kingdom against you this season will come to nothing in Jesus's name.

> Believers must be active participants in the spiritual realm. Praying for one hour at night has great effects on the operations of the dark kingdom, much more all night prayer. Reduce your sleep! As they meet to determine your fate, you go on your knees and determine theirs, scatter their meeting and strip them powerless.[3]

Midnight is also the witching hour, the time of day when supernatural creatures such as witches, demons, and ghosts are thought to appear and be at their most powerful, and black magic at its most effective. This hour is typically past midnight or the time in the middle of the night when magic things are said to happen.

> At midnight I will rise to give thanks to You, because of Your righteous judgments.
>
> —Psalm 119:62

In Psalm 91:6 the psalmist mentions the pestilence that walks in darkness: "Nor of the pestilence that walks in darkness, nor of the destruction that lays waste at noonday." This is a picture of evil walking at night.

Midnight speaks of darkness—the absence of light and the presence of blindness. It is for rest and is unsuitable for labor. It is favorable to the purposes of wickedness. Wild beasts seek their prey at night. Shepherds watch over their sheep at night. The midnight is a period of severe calamities. Darkness has binding powers and limits activities. It has separating powers. That is when all that is evil and unworthy of light is let loose. But the enemy does not own the night; the night belongs to God: "The day is Yours, the *night* also is Yours; You have prepared the light and the sun" (Ps. 74:16, emphasis added).

Mark 1:35 tells us that Jesus prayed at night: "And in the morning, rising up a great while before day, he went out, and departed into a solitary place, and there prayed" (KJV). He is our example of how to stay connected to God, free from unbelief, and remain in the power of the supernatural and miracles.

Midnight is a great and strategic time to pray. Midnight represents the darkness of the night. Night is symbolic of darkness and the time when men are sleeping. The enemy likes to plan and work when men are sleeping, so rising up at night in prayer will definitely thwart and interrupt his plans.

MIDDAY PRAYER

The whole idea of praying at 12:00 p.m. (midday) is that it allows God to interrupt your day. Whether or not you already have a regular time of prayer, disciplining yourself to pray in the center of your day means your mind returns to God regardless of the pressures or busyness of daily life.

> Nor of the pestilence that walks in darkness, nor of the destruction that lays waste at noonday.
>
> —PSALM 91:6

There is also an opportunity to pray against the midday curse. Deuteronomy 28:29 says that "at midday you will grope about like a blind man in the dark. You will be unsuccessful in everything you do; day after day you will be oppressed and robbed, with no one to rescue you" (NIV). This is the plan of the enemy at work. We can establish a defense against this vicious plan by seeking God and praying against the enemy at noon.

Noon is the high point of the day and the sun. The sun is responsible for warmth and prosperity. "High noon" is defined as the most advanced, flourishing, or creative stage or period. *High* means "elevated above any starting point of measurement, as a line, or surface; having altitude; lifted up; raised or extended in the direction of the zenith; lofty; tall; as, a high mountain, tower, tree; the sun is high." Synonyms for *high noon* include:

> acme, apex, apogee, brow, cap, climax, cloud nine, crest, crown, culmen, culmination, edge, eight bells, extreme limit, extremity, heaven, heavens, height, highest pitch, highest point, limit, maximum, meridian, meridiem, midday, mountaintop, ne plus ultra, no place higher, noon, noonday, nooning, noonlight, noontide, noontime, peak, pinnacle, pitch, point, pole, ridge, seventh heaven, sky, spire, summit, tip, tip-top, top, upmost, upper extremity, uppermost, utmost, vertex, very top, zenith.[4]

Noon prophetically represents a high point. Pray high things at noon. Pray to be lifted higher in the things of God and the Spirit.

PRAYERS TO RELEASE THE MORNING AND THE DAYSPRING

Lord, You command the morning and cause the dayspring to know his place. Let all wickedness be shaken out of my life, in the name of Jesus (Job 38:12–13).

Let the morning and the dayspring arise in my life.

Let the dew of the morning be upon my life, in the name of Jesus.

Let the blessing of the morning arise in my life, in the name of Jesus.

Let the Sun of righteousness arise with healing in his wings, and let every area of my life be healed, in the name of Jesus.

Lord, You are a sun and a shield for my life. Withhold no good thing from my life.

With this new morning let new mercy and favor be upon my life, in the name of Jesus.

Jesus, You are my Dayspring; release more light and revelation into my life.

Dayspring, take Your place in my life.

Dayspring from on high, visit me.

Let wickedness be shaken out of my family, city, region, and nation, in the name of Jesus.

Let the wicked scatter as the dayspring takes his place.

Dayspring, take hold of the ends of the earth and root out wickedness.

Dayspring, take hold of the ends of the earth and drive out darkness.

Nothing is hidden from You, Lord, for You created the dayspring.

Let there be a new dawning in my life, in the name of Jesus.

I praise You, Lord, in the morning.

Let Your name be praised from the rising of the sun to the going down of the same (Ps. 113:3).

PRAYERS TO RELEASE THE MERCY AND FAVOR OF THE MORNING

Cause me to hear Your lovingkindness in the morning; for in You do I trust. Cause me to know the way that I should walk, for I lift up my soul to You (Ps. 143:8).

I will sing of Your power; yes, I will sing aloud of Your mercy in the morning. You have been my defense and refuge in the day of my trouble (Ps. 59:16).

Show forth Your lovingkindness in the morning and Your faithfulness every night (Ps. 92:2).

Because of Your mercy, Lord, I am not consumed. Your compassions never fail. They are new every morning. Great is Your faithfulness (Lam. 3:22–23).

Lord, You are my sun and shield. You give me grace and glory and will withhold no good thing from me (Ps. 84:11).

Lord, You are a sun and shield; let my life be protected by You in the day and the night.

Prayers to Release the Blessing of High Noon

Let the blessing of the sun be upon my life.

Let me experience a great and joyful harvest, in the name of Jesus (Deut. 33:14).

Lord, the day is Yours and the night also. You have prepared the light and the sun (Ps. 74:16).

The Lord God is my strength. He will make my feet like hinds' feet and will make me to walk on my high places (Hab. 3:19).

Also now, behold, my witness is in heaven, and my record is on high (Job 16:19).

The Lord is my rock, fortress, and deliverer; He is my God, my strength, in whom I will trust. He is my buckler, the horn of my salvation, and my high tower (Ps. 18:2).

He makes my feet like the feet of deer and sets me on my high places (Ps. 18:33).

From the end of the earth I will cry to You, when my heart is overwhelmed; lead me to the rock that is higher than I (Ps. 61:2).

I am poor and sorrowful; let Your salvation, O God, set me up on high (Ps. 69:29).

The Highest Himself shall establish me (Ps. 87:5).

I dwell in the secret place of the Most High and abide under the shadow of the Almighty (Ps. 91:1).

Because I have set my love upon Him, He will deliver me; He will set me on high because I have known His name (Ps. 91:14).

He has set me on high from affliction and makes my family like a flock (Ps. 107:41).

I will dwell on high; my place of defense shall be the fortress of rocks. Bread shall be given me, and my waters shall be sure (Isa. 33:16).

A highway will be there for me—a way—and it shall be called the way of holiness. The unclean will not pass over it, but I will walk along this highway and will not go astray (Isa. 35:8).

I will get up into the high mountain. I will lift my voice and say to the cities, "Behold your God" (Isa. 40:9).

The Lord will open to me the rivers in high places and fountains in the midst of the valleys. He will make the wilderness a pool of water and the dry land springs of water (Isa. 41:18).

I will feed along the road, and my pasture will be in all high places (Isa. 49:9).

God will make my mountains a road, and my highways will be elevated (Isa. 49:11).

Lord, I surrender to Your ways; for as the heavens are higher than the earth, so are Your ways higher than mine and Your thoughts than my thoughts (Isa. 55:9).

PRAYERS TO REDEEM FROM THE CURSE AT MIDDAY

I am redeemed from the curse at midday (Deut. 28:29).

I am redeemed from destruction at midday (Ps. 91:6).

I will praise and pray at midday (Ps. 55:17).

The sun will not smite me by day (Ps. 121:6).

The sun will bless my life. My life will be fruitful (Deut. 33:13–16).

I will not be vain or vexed under the sun (Eccles. 1:14).

I will love and enjoy life under the sun (Eccles. 2:17)

I will not be oppressed under the sun; I have the Comforter—the Holy Spirit (Eccles. 4:1).

DECLARATIONS AGAINST THE OPERATION OF EVIL AT NIGHT

I bind and rebuke anything operating against me at night, in the name of Jesus.

I will not be tormented at night.

Anything operating under the cover of darkness, be exposed, in the name of Jesus.

Darkness will not overwhelm my life, but I have the light of life.

I will not be afraid of the terror at night.

Let every prison door be opened, and let every foundation of wickedness be shaken.

Lord, release Your angels of deliverance for me, in the name of Jesus.

The day and the night belong to You, Lord; let me be blessed in the day and the night.

You created the day and the night for Your pleasure, Lord. Let me enjoy the day and the night.

CHAPTER 7

PRAYER AND FASTING

> Then the disciples came to Jesus privately and said, "Why could we not cast him out?" So Jesus said to them, "Because of your unbelief; for assuredly, I say to you, if you have faith as a mustard seed, you will say to this mountain, 'Move from here to there,' and it will move; and nothing will be impossible for you. However, this kind does not go out except by prayer and fasting."
>
> —MATTHEW 17:19–21

UNBELIEF IS AN enemy to overcoming mountains of what seems to be impossible. In Matthew 13:58 we find that Jesus did not operate in the power of God in His hometown because of the unbelief of the people. The disciples could not cast out a strong demon because of unbelief.

It is important to drive unbelief from your life. And one of the ways this is accomplished is through prayer and fasting. Prayer and fasting help us clear obstacles to our faith and faith-filled actions.

Fasting, coupled with prayer, is one of the most powerful weapons to receiving a breakthrough and overcoming unbelief. Jesus preceded His ministry with fasting and returned in the power of the Spirit into Galilee. Jesus did not struggle with unbelief, and He operated in faith throughout His ministry. When you are challenged with unbelief in any situation, I encourage you to fast and pray for breakthrough.

FASTING RELEASES THE BREAKER ANOINTING

What are your mountains? In the introduction I named many of the common mountains we all face at different seasons in our lives. Maybe you've been praying over these things for a long time and have not seen breakthrough.

In Micah 2:13 the prophet prophesied, "The one who breaks open will come up before them; they will break out, pass through the gate, and go out by it; their king will pass before them, with the LORD at their head." We are living in the days of the breaker. The Lord is the breaker. He is able to break through any obstacle, opposition, or mountain on behalf of His people. There is a breaker anointing arising upon the church. We will see and experience more breakthroughs than ever before.

Fasting is one of the ways to increase the breaker anointing. Fasting will cause breakthroughs in families, cities, nations, finances, church growth, salvation, healing, and deliverance. Fasting will help you to break through the toughest situations. Fasting will help you to break through all opposition of the enemy.

There are some spirits in a person, region, or nation that cannot be overcome without fasting. Many believers struggle with certain limitations they cannot seem to break through. A revelation of fasting will change this and result in victories that would not be ordinarily obtained. A life of consistent fasting will cause many victories to manifest. God's will is that every believer live a life of victory with nothing being impossible.

There are stubborn spirits that will respond only to fasting and prayer. These tend to be generational strongholds that tenaciously hold on to families and nations for years. Fasting will break these strongholds. These strongholds include poverty, sickness, witchcraft, sexual impurity, pride, fear, confusion, and marital problems. Do any of these sound like the mountains you are facing today? Fasting will help you overcome these strongholds and break free from their limitations.

> But you, when you fast, anoint your head and wash your face, so that you do not appear to men to be fasting, but to your Father who is in the secret place; and your Father who sees in secret will reward you openly.
>
> —Matthew 6:17–18

Fasting breaks the mountain of the spirit of poverty (Joel 2:15, 18–19).

Joel gave the people of Israel the proper response to the locust invasion. Locusts represent demons that devour. Locusts represent the spirits of poverty and lack. The locust had come upon Israel and devoured the harvest. Joel encouraged the people to fast and repent. God promised to hear their prayer and answer by sending corn, wine, and oil.

Corn, wine, and oil represent prosperity. Fasting breaks the spirit of poverty and releases the spirit of prosperity. I have seen countless numbers of believers struggle in the area of their finances. Prosperity is elusive to many. This mountain of poverty can be moved through fasting and prayer.

Fasting breaks the mountain of fear and releases great things (Joel 2:21).

Do you desire to see great things happen in your life? The Lord desires to do great things for His people. Fasting prepares the way for great things to happen. These great things include signs and wonders.

Fasting causes us to become more fruitful (Joel 2:22).

Fasting increases the fruit of a believer's life. This includes the fruit of the Spirit. God desires His people to be more fruitful. Fasting helps our ministries become more fruitful.

Fasting releases the rain (Joel 2:23).

Rain represents the outpouring of the Holy Spirit. Rain also represents blessing and refreshing. Israel needed the former rain to moisten the ground for planting. They needed the latter rain to bring the crops to maturity. God has promised to give the former and latter rains in response to fasting.

Fasting moistens the ground (the heart) for the planting of the seed (the Word of God). Fasting causes the rain to fall in dry places. Nations and cities that have not experienced revival can receive rain through fasting.

Fasting releases the Holy Spirit and increases the prophetic anointing (Joel 2:28).

Fasting helps to release one of the greatest promises given by the prophet Joel. This is the promise of the last-day outpouring of the Holy Spirit. Fasting helps to release the manifestation of prophecy. Fasting also helps release visions and dreams.

Fasting breaks the mountain of sexual impurity (Judg. 19:22–20:5).

Sexual sin is one of the hardest sins to break. Many believers struggle with generational lust. Lust spirits cause much shame, guilt, and condemnation. This robs the believer of the confidence and boldness he should have. Many believers struggle with masturbation, pornography, perversion, and fornication. Fasting will help drive these spirits from a person's life.

Fasting brings enlargement and deliverance (Esther 4:14–16).

Fasting was a part of defeating Haman's plans to destroy the Jews. The whole nation of Israel was delivered because of fasting. Esther needed favor from the king and received it as a result of fasting. Fasting releases favor and brings great deliverance.

The Jews not only defeated their enemies, but they were also enlarged. Mordecai was promoted and Haman was hung. Enlargement comes through fasting. Fasting breaks limitations and gives you more room to expand and grow. God desires to enlarge our borders (Deut. 12:20). God wants us to have more territory. This includes natural and spiritual territory. Fasting breaks limitations and causes expansion.

Fasting breaks the mountain of sickness and infirmity and releases healing (Isa. 58:5–6, 8).

Many believers struggle with sicknesses such as cancer, diabetes, high blood pressure, sinus problems, and chronic pain. These spirits of infirmity are often generational. Fasting helps eliminate chronic sicknesses and diseases. God has promised that our health will spring forth speedily.

Fasting releases God's glory for our protection (Isa. 58:8).

Divine protection is another promise from Isaiah 58. God promises to protect us with His glory. Fasting releases the glory of the Lord that covers us. God has promised to cover the church with glory as a defense (Isa. 4:5). The enemy cannot penetrate or overcome this glory.

Fasting results in answered prayer (Isa. 58:9).

Demonic interference causes many prayers to be hindered. Daniel fasted twenty-one days to break through demonic resistance and receive answers to his prayers. The prince of Persia withstood the answers for twenty-one days. Daniel's fast helped an angel to break through and bring the answers.

Fasting will cause many answers to prayer to be accelerated. These include prayers for salvation of loved ones and deliverance. Fasting helps to break the frustration of unanswered prayer.

Fasting releases divine guidance (Isa. 58:11).

Many believers have difficulty making correct decisions concerning relationships, finances, and ministry. This causes setbacks and wasted time because of foolish decisions. Fasting will help believers make correct decisions by releasing divine guidance. Fasting eliminates confusion. Fasting causes clarity and releases understanding and wisdom to make correct decisions.

Fasting is recommended for those who are making important decisions such as marriage and ministry choices.

Fasting breaks generational mountains and curses (Isa. 58:12).

Many of the obstacles that believers encounter are generational. Generational curses result from the iniquity of the fathers. Generational sins such as pride, rebellion, idolatry, witchcraft, occult involvement, Masonry, and lust open the door for evil spirits to operate in families through generations. Demons of destruction, failure, poverty, infirmity, lust, and addiction are major strongholds in the lives of millions of people.

Fasting helps loose the bands of wickedness. Fasting lets the oppressed go free. Fasting helps us to rebuild the old waste places. Fasting reverses the desolation that results from sin and rebellion.

Fasting closes the breaches and brings forth restoration (Isa. 58:12).

There are many believers who need restoration. They need restoration in their families, finances, relationships, health, and walk with the Lord. Fasting is a part of restoration.

Fasting closes the breaches. Breaches are gaps in the wall that give the enemy an entry point into our lives. Breaches need to be repaired and closed. When the breaches are closed, the enemy no longer has an opening to attack.

Fasting restores the ancient paths (Isa. 58:12).

Fasting helps keep us on the right path. Fasting helps to prevent us from going astray. Fasting will help those who have strayed from the right path to return. Fasting is a cure for backsliding. Fasting will help restore us to the right path.

Fasting helps us to walk in the good path (Prov. 2:9),

the path of life (v. 19), the path of peace (Prov. 3:17), the old path (Jer. 6:16), and the straight path (Heb. 12:13). Fasting restores these paths and helps us to walk in them.

Fasting causes you to have great victory against overwhelming odds (2 Chron. 20:3).

Jehoshaphat was facing the combined armies of Moab, Ammon, and Edom. He was facing overwhelming odds. Fasting helped him to defeat these enemies. Fasting helps us to have victory in the midst of defeat.

Jehoshaphat called a fast because he was afraid. Fear is another stronghold that many believers have difficulty overcoming. Fasting will break the power of the demon of fear. Spirits of terror, panic, fright, apprehension, and timidity can be overcome through fasting. Freedom from fear is a requirement to live a victorious lifestyle.

Fasting prepares the way for you and your children and delivers you from enemies that lie in wait (Ezra 8:21, 31).

Ezra fasted because he recognized the danger of his mission. Fasting will protect you and your children from the plans of the enemy. Fasting will stop the ambush of the enemy. Fasting will cause your substance to be protected from the attack of the enemy.

Fasting breaks the mountains of pride, rebellion, and witchcraft (Ps. 35:13; Job 33:17–20).

Sickness can be the result of pride. Pain can also be the result of pride. Sickness often results in the loss of appetite. This is a forced fast. Fasting humbles the soul.

Fasting helps us overcome the strongman of pride. Pride and rebellion are generational spirits that are often difficult to overcome.

Gluttony and drunkenness are signs of rebellion (Deut. 21:20). Rebellion is as the sin of witchcraft (1 Sam. 15:23). God humbled Israel in the wilderness by feeding them with only manna (Deut. 8:3). Israel lusted for meat in the wilderness. This was a manifestation of rebellion (Ps. 106:14–15).

Fasting causes the joy and presence of the Lord to return (Mark 2:20).

The presence of the bridegroom causes joy. Weddings are filled with joy and celebration. When a believer loses the joy and presence of the Lord, he or she needs to fast. Fasting causes the joy and presence of the Lord to return. No believer can live a victorious life without the presence of the Bridegroom.

Fasting releases the power of the Holy Spirit for the miraculous (Luke 4:14, 18).

Fasting increases the anointing and the power of the Holy Spirit in a person's life. Jesus ministered in power after fasting. He healed the sick and cast out devils. All believers are expected to do the same works (John 14:12). Fasting helps us to walk in the power of God. Fasting releases the anointing for miracles.

Fasting Must Be Genuine, Not Religious or Hypocritical

In Luke 18:11–12 the Pharisee fasted with attitudes of pride and superiority. These attitudes are not acceptable to God. God requires humility and sincerity in fasting. We must have the correct motives in fasting. Fasting is a powerful tool if done correctly. Fasting cannot be done religiously or hypocritically.

Isaiah 58 describes the fast that God had chosen. Fasting cannot be done with amusement (v. 3). Fasting cannot be done while mistreating others (v. 3). Fasting cannot be done for strife and contention (v. 4). Fasting causes one to bow his head like a bulrush (v. 5). Fasting must be done in humility. Fasting is a time of searching the heart and repenting. Fasting must be done in an attitude of compassion for the lost and hurting (v. 7). This is the fast that God promises to bless.

The enemy knows the power of prayer and fasting, and he will do everything in his power to stop you. Believers who begin to fast can expect much spiritual resistance. You must be committed to a fasted lifestyle. The rewards of fasting far outweigh the obstacles of the enemy. A revelation of the power of fasting will help you to break through!

PRAYERS AGAINST STUBBORN DEMONS AND STRONGHOLDS*

I bind, rebuke, and cast out every stubborn demon that would attempt to stubbornly hold on to my life in the name of Jesus.

I come against every stubborn stronghold and command it to yield to the power of God and the name of Jesus (2 Sam. 5:7).

I put pressure on every stubborn demon and stronghold and break its grip in my life, in the name of Jesus.

I uproot every stubborn root from my life, in the name of Jesus (Matt. 15:13).

I command every stubborn, ironlike yoke to shatter and break, in the name of Jesus (Judg. 1:19).

I break the power of every proud, stubborn, and arrogant demon that exalts itself against Christ, and I command it to be abased, in the name of Jesus.

In the name of Jesus, I break the power of all iniquity in my family that would stubbornly attempt to control my life.

I come against all obstinate demons, and break their influence in my life in the name of Jesus.

---

* These prayers coupled with fasting and deliverance will bring breakthrough (Matt. 17:21).

I rebuke all stubborn, habitual patterns of failure and frustration in my life in the name of Jesus.

I rebuke all stubborn pharaohs that would attempt to hold God's people, and I command you to let God's people go, in the name of Jesus (Exod. 8:32).

In the name of Jesus, I bind and rebuke all stubborn enemies, who stubbornly oppose me and my progress.

I rebuke all stubborn demons that would attempt to resist the power of God and the authority I have through Jesus Christ, and I render you powerless to resist, in the name of Jesus.

I come against every persistent pattern that limits me, and I render it powerless against me, in the name of Jesus.

There is nothing impossible through faith. I release my faith against every stubborn and obstinate demon, and I resist you steadfastly, in the name of Jesus (Matt. 19:26).

I weaken, break down, and pressure every stubborn demon and stronghold; you are getting weaker and weaker, and I am getting stronger and stronger.

I exercise long war against all stubborn demons until you are completely defeated and destroyed from my life, in the name of Jesus (2 Sam. 3:1).

I lay siege against every stubborn stronghold through prayer and fasting, until your walls come down, in the name of Jesus (Deut. 20:19).

I use the battering ram of prayer and fasting to demolish all the gates of every stubborn stronghold, in the name of Jesus.

Let every Jericho wall fall through my praise, as I lift my voice as a trumpet against you, in the name of Jesus (Josh. 6:1, 20).

Let every demonic stump be removed from my life, in the name of Jesus.

In the name of Jesus, I break the will of every stubborn spirit that would attempt to remain in my life.

I speak to every stubborn demon: You have no will to remain, your will is broken, and you must submit to the name of Jesus and the power of the Holy Ghost.

I come against all stubborn demons and strongholds in my family that have refused to leave, and in the name of Jesus, I assault every demonic fortress that has been built for generations.

I rebuke every stubborn mule and bull of Bashan from my life, in the name of Jesus.

In the name of Jesus, I break the will of every stubborn mule that comes against me. You are defeated and must bow to the name above all names (Ps. 22:12).

The anointing is increasing in my life through prayer and fasting, and every stubborn yoke is being destroyed (Isa. 10:27).

NOTES

CHAPTER 1
THE PRAYER OF FAITH

1. Larry Keefauver, ed., *The Original John G. Lake Devotional* (Lake Mary, FL: Charisma House, 1997), 149.

2. Ibid., 149–150.

3. Larry Keefauver, ed., *The Original Azusa Street Devotional* (Lake Mary, FL: Charisma House, 1997), 119–120.

4. Kenneth E. Hagin, "Gift of Faith and the Working of Miracles," cFaith.com, http://www.cfaith.com/index .php?option=com_content&view=article&id=1171:gift-of -faith-and-the-working-of-miracles&catid=45:faith&Itemid=91 (accessed March 14, 2012).

CHAPTER 3
THE PERSISTENT PRAYER

1. Merriam-Webster.com, Dictionary, s.v. "persist," http://www .merriam-webster.com/dictionary/persist (accessed April 17, 2012).

2. Merriam-Webster.com, Thesaurus, s.v. "persist," http://www .merriam-webster.com/thesaurus/persist (accessed April 17, 2012).

3. Keefauver, ed., *The Original Azusa Street Devotional*, 102.

CHAPTER 5
THE PRAYER OF THE DESTITUTE

1. Merriam-Webster.com, Dictionary, s.v. "destitute," http://www .merriam-webster.com/dictionary/destitute (accessed April 18, 2012).

2. *Barnes' Notes*, electronic database, s.v. "Ps. 102:17," PC Study Bible, copyright © 1997 Biblesoft.

3. Webster's Online Dictionary, s.v. "Common Expressions: Fortuna," http://www.websters-online-dictionary.org/definitions /Fortuna?cx=partner-pub-0939450753529744%3Av0qd01 -tdlq&cof=FORID%3A9&ie=UTF-8&q=Fortuna&sa=Search#906 (accessed April 18, 2012).

4. Wikipedia.org, s.v. "Rota Fortunae," http://en.wikipedia.org /wiki/The_Wheel_of_Fortune_(medieval) (accessed April 18, 2012).

5. KJVToday.com, "'Troop/Number' or 'Fortune (Gad)/Destiny (Meni)" in Isaiah 55:11?", http://www.kjvtoday.com/home /troopnumber-or-fortune-gaddestiny-meni-in-isaiah-6511 (acessed April 18, 2012).

CHAPTER 6
MIDNIGHT AND MIDDAY PRAYER

1. Sr. Eleanor, "Vigils: Prayer During the Darkness of Night," *Cistercian Vocation* (blog), June 22, 2008, http:// cistercianvocation.wordpress.com/2008/06/22/vigils-prayer -during-the-darkness-of-night/ (accessed April 18, 2012).

2. *Adam Clarke's Commentary*, electronic database, s.v. "Psalm 42:8," PC Study Bible, copyright © 1996 Biblesoft.

3. Pasor E. Adeboye, "Night Vigil," SolidRockDublin.org, February 22, 2011, http://solidrockdublin.org/?p=1417 (accessed March 27, 2012).

4. *Moby Thesaurus*, s.v. "high noon," Babylon.com, http:// thesaurus.babylon.com/high%20noon (accessed April 19, 2012).